A BACKWARD LOOK

Germans Remember

A BACKWARD

LOOK

by Daniel Lang

McGRAW-HILL BOOK COMPANY

New York   St. Louis   San Francisco
Düsseldorf   London   Mexico   Sydney   Toronto

895

LIBRARY OF CONGRESS CATALOGING IN PUBLICATION DATA

Lang, Daniel.
    A backward look.
    1. Germany—History—1933–1945. 2. World
War, 1939–1945—Public opinion—Germany.
3. Public opinion—Germany. I. Title.
DD256.5.L36   943.086   78-10326
ISBN 0-07-036239-4

A substantial portion of this book appeared in *The New Yorker*.

Book design by Marsha Picker

CREDITS FOR FIRST PICTURE SECTION (following p. 22): All photographs
courtesy Paul Emunds except: photograph on first page from *Mit 15 an die
Kanonen;* photograph on fourth page courtesy Meinrad Emunds; photographs on fifth page courtesy Franz Josef Emunds (top) and courtesy
Kaiser-Karls-Gymnasium (bottom).
CREDITS FOR SECOND PICTURE SECTION (following p. 44): All photographs
courtesy Paul Emunds except: photographs on fourth page (bottom) and
fifth page (bottom) courtesy Meinrad Emunds; photographs on sixth,
eighth, and ninth pages courtesy German Information Center, New York;
photograph on seventh page courtesy Selfhelp Community Services,
New York.

To my grandchildren,
present and future

ALSO BY DANIEL LANG

Early Tales of the Atomic Age

The Man in the Thick Lead Suit

From Hiroshima to the Moon

An Inquiry into Enoughness

Casualties of War

Patriotism without Flags

For children (fiction)

A Summer's Duckling

This book could not have been written without the help of Annemarie Levitt.

I am indebted to William Whitworth for his editing.

D. L.

Contents

To the Cannons at Fifteen I

From time to time, Germans of my acquaintance have mentioned that there is little disposition in their country to recall the days of Hitler's Third Reich. Some of them have cited as evidence the fact that the Germans—the principal actors in one of history's most horrendous chapters—have contributed but a trickle to the international torrent of books, plays, films, and scholarly studies dealing with *der Führer*'s rise and fall. Since his suicide, in 1945, I have often wondered what Germans, looking back, make of his regime, and recently, despite their reputed reluctance to reminisce, I talked about it with a number of them in their country. I had had this idea since the war, but, oddly, I wasn't prompted to act on it until I heard of a high-school assignment that a history teacher in the Rhineland border town of Aachen had given his students—all boys of fifteen. The instructor, Paul Emunds, a fifty-three-year-old faculty member of long standing at the Kaiser-Karls-Gymnasium, had been lecturing about the Third Reich one morning in 1974 when, looking at the still unformed faces of his adolescent listeners, it came back to him that there had been a time, in 1943 and 1944, when similar fifteen-year-olds, from the Kaiser-Karls-Gymnasium and other Aachen schools, were pressed into military service as *Flakhelfer*—that is, as anti-aircraft helpers. The boys had been assigned to six batteries ringing the city and commanded by Luftwaffe personnel, nearly all of whom had been ordered to the border town from other parts of Germany. As Emunds told me when we met, the recollection had given him an idea for a class project—namely, to bring together his students and these ex-*Flakhelfer*, now middle-aged, like him. Such an encounter, the teacher thought, would give the students a far more vivid sense of the war than he himself could ever hope to impart.

2   Emunds, who had been an Aachener all his life, knew that plenty of ex-*Flakhelfer*—there had been seven hundred and seventy-eight—continued to live in the vicinity, as did a handful of former Luftwaffe men who had been their superiors. Then, too, Emunds foresaw,

the project held out the possibility of a nice little field trip for his students: they could go to Koblenz, ninety-five miles to the southeast, where, he knew, government archives contained further data about the Kaiser Karl boys of decades ago.

The plan worked out well, despite an initial wariness on the part of the school administration. The K.K.G., as townspeople refer to the Kaiser-Karls-Gymnasium, is traditionalist in outlook, relying heavily on the teaching of classics. Founded in 1601, it is named for Charlemagne, whom Germans call Karl der Grosse, and it occupies a somber brown three-story stone building that lies in the shadow of Aachen's cathedral, where Charlemagne was crowned King of the Franks in 768; the ruler spent much of his time in Aachen, a spa that is familiar to the nearby Belgians and French as Aix-la-Chapelle. In any event, once the school administration had agreed to Emunds' unusual project, his students carried out their tasks diligently, handing in copious reports, thanks to the ready cooperation of former *Flakhelfer* as well as the parents of some of these alumni, most of them now grandparents and well into their seventies. In all, the boys saw a hundred and forty-seven people. At Koblenz, the archives proved a model of thoroughness, yielding a welter of statistics, among them the information that the youthful gunners' helpers had assisted in the downing of as many as a hundred Allied planes. To Emunds' gratification, the school administration's approbation was forthcoming, but as things turned out Emunds had even more than this to

3

show for his enterprise. Pleased with the material gathered under his supervision, he decided to put it together as a paperback, confident that it would make an interesting memento for students and parents; any proceeds from the book would go for such purposes as restocking the school library or inviting poets to give readings of their verse. When two public-spirited organizations agreed to underwrite the book's publication, Emunds began editing his students' reports and shaping them into a whole; he also found a university professor to write an introduction and dug up a collection of photographs that some *Flakhelfer* themselves had taken during the war. One of the photographs showed a classroom scene in which a benign-looking teacher of English was bidding farewell to departing *Flakhelfer;* behind the teacher was a blackboard on which he had scrawled, in English, "Who can say what tomorrow will bring?"

The book finally came out in late 1975, bearing the title *Mit 15 an die Kanonen (To the Cannons at Fifteen)*. To Emunds' astonishment, its appearance was greeted as an event, small but definite. "It seemed to touch a nerve," Emunds told me. Within weeks of publication, orders had been received for more than five thousand copies. Scores of letters poured in to the teacher, all of which he put in a scrapbook. German newspapers and television stations reported the high-school assignment extensively, and so did the international press, including the New York *Times*. In the school lobby, as I was to see for myself, a glass case displayed dozens of clippings, one of them headed in part *"Der Blick Zurück"* ("The Backward Look"). As for me, I wrote to Emunds shortly after learning about *Mit 15 an die Kanonen.* Here, it seemed to me, might well be a German who was prepared to look back at the Nazi past. In my letter, I told Emunds about my long-standing notion of recalling the war with Germans, and he responded warmly, offering to give me as much time as I might want; in addition, he said, he would arrange for me to talk not only with *Flakhelfer* and others who had been interviewed but with the interviewers themselves—his students, that is, who had now turned seventeen and were about to graduate. He would be most interested, Emunds said, to see what would come of a foreigner's visit.

Before my departure for Germany, Emunds sent me a copy of *Mit 15 an die Kanonen.* It was three hundred and eleven pages long, and its price was twelve marks—just under five dollars. Primarily, the book was a compendium of depositions, occasionally contradictory, with excerpts arranged under such chapter titles as "Now They Are Calling Children," "Student Soldiers—Soldier Students," "Youth Under Fire," "The Americans Are Coming," and, finally, "Thirty Years Later." The book followed no particular pattern. Interspersed at random among the excerpts were commentaries by Emunds' students, sections of official wartime documents, and tables of figures from which it was possible to glean such disparate facts as the number of air-raid alarms sounded in Aachen and the cubic meters of rubble per capita resulting from Allied bombings. Mention is made, too, of a clock in a church steeple that was shocked out of commission by the near misses of enemy bombs on April 11, 1944, at twenty minutes of midnight; it wasn't until years after the war ended that repairmen set the clock's hands moving again.

Both the content and the tone of *Mit 15 an die Kanonen* struck me as curious. The book had an air of careful detachment that I hadn't expected. I had imagined that as long as the former anti-aircraft helpers had consented to recall the war, they would give vent to feelings about it that might have lain dormant for thirty years. The men had nothing to fear in the way of publicity, for they were quoted anonymously. ("Otherwise, they would not have spoken as freely as they did," Emunds explained when we met.) Even under this condition, however, and even after the passage of thirty years, no outcry against Hitler and his deeds is forthcoming from any of the book's contributors. Indeed, *der Führer's* name is rarely mentioned. And nowhere does one come upon any forthright expression of feeling concerning concentration camps and gas chambers; in fact, they are scarcely referred to. At one point, the book speaks of "rumors [*Gerüchte*] about the persecution of the Jewish people," and at another an isolated incident is recounted in which a student at the K.K.G. was unable to listen silently to a lecture about the "inferiority" of Jews that was being delivered by a history teacher. "The Jews are also human beings," the student had blurted out. Distracted, the teacher had looked up from his papers momentarily, and then, to everyone's surprise, he had carried on with his lecture as though nothing had happened.

In the book, the enemy, meaning the Allies, comes through as a linear tormentor, his single motive for going to war being the destruction of Aachen and the rest of the Fatherland. In one of the book's commentaries, a K.K.G. researcher states that written material he has come across persuades him that a belief is currently prevalent among Germans that it was England that "started aerial warfare against civilians" by attacking German "residential areas." Elsewhere in the book, a *Flakhelfer* tells of seeing the body of a British pilot—his first corpse—which led the then schoolboy to ruminate, "We were shooting at human beings; that was something we had never taken into account." A different tone is heard in a *Flakhelfer*'s description of a day when he and his fellows were having gunnery practice. A perfect target had come into view: a crippled American plane. In no time, it was a plummeting torch, and one of its crew, bailing out, parachuted to the ground, where townspeople fell upon him; he was rescued and made a prisoner of war. One reads, "More and more there developed a ... hatred of the cowardly attacks from the air," and "In spite of the devastating effects of the terror bombing, the Allies did not succeed in setting the German people against their leaders." Another of Emunds' interviewees declared that on completing his stint as a *Flakhelfer* he felt "proud" of having assisted in the downing of fifty-two planes. He says, "When we saw the dead comrades in our battery ... we thought, You've taken away our comrades, and for that we'll shoot at you now better than ever. We saw our home town burning and smoldering and turned into rubble and ashes, and that created rage in us."

This note of indomitability is sounded repeatedly. Indeed, if the book does have a crowning reflection, it is embodied in the statement "All in all, it will remain a historical truth that a people cannot be conquered by terror." Repeatedly, too, one finds *Flakhelfer* looking back on their anti-aircraft days as having been "idealistic." "We were hopeless idealists," one *Flakhelfer* states; one of the noncommissioned officers notes that "German idealism has always been a great, great problem." The observation is also entered that the end of the war meant "[going from being idealists] to becoming virtual nihilists, saying, 'Everything [we believed in] has gone *kaputt.*'" A section of the book deals with the question whether being a *Flakhelfer* was a good experience, and in effect a single reservation is offered: retrospectively, it is said, like other demands of the dictatorship, the experience tended to kill any appetite for thinking. "To think—that we learned only after the war," a *Flakhelfer* remarks. Apart from this reservation, the response to the query is a positive one. The book states that "for many, the 'act of service' was above all an opportunity ... of proving themselves to their parents and other adults." One deponent in *Mit 15 an die Kanonen* suggests that being a *Flakhelfer* may have made him prematurely self-reliant; now the father of a fifteen-year-old son, he suspects that this may explain his tendency to be "somewhat rough" (*etwas grob*) as a parent. "The experience formed me," one reads. "I learned a lot that I most definitely would not have learned otherwise. ... I made demands on myself and as a result could handle . . . difficult situations." Consistently, it is found, the responses emphasize the unquestioned value of a *Flakhelfer* past, and among the advantages claimed for precocious military service are that, besides hastening the onset of manhood, it heightens one's sense of patriotism, makes for lasting friendships, and, praise be, does away with the bother of attending school. The *Gymnasium* students, though, did not entirely escape classes, for, like circuit riders, teachers went from one anti-aircraft station to another to drill the boys in Latin, history, and other subjects. The visits were deflating to the boys. Strutting in pale-blue uniforms, they were proud of not being separated from the men. They were constantly on the lookout for insignia, to which they were entitled but which weren't easy to come by, owing to an acute shortage of metal. One *Flakhelfer* recalls that to overcome this he and some friends stole spoons from home, delivering them for refashioning to a Luftwaffe man, a Viennese, who had been a medal-maker in civilian life. In *Mit 15 an die Kanonen,* one K.K.G. alumnus relates that he and his classmates "erupted into a dance of joy" when word reached them that bombs had partly demolished their school. The book also discloses that on more than one occasion, in return for cigarettes, Luftwaffe sergeants obligingly set off false air-raid alarms to keep the boys' teachers from making their rounds. Conceivably, the sergeants might have done as much without bribes, for the Luftwaffe was a Nazi innovation, and its personnel, far more than that of the Army or the Navy, reflected the regime's animosity toward book learning as well as toward religion. In the seemingly distant time of the Third Reich, one finds in the paperback, "Christian morality" (*Christliche Sittlichkeit*) was employed as a term of derision. As for book learning, Luftwaffe personnel had little inhibition in giving visiting teachers short shrift. On one occasion, Emunds' book tells us, a sergeant, pulling rank on a teacher, halted a math lesson and, grinning, commanded his young charges to watch a light, frothy film. On record, too, is a letter in which a lieutenant reminds the director of an Aachen school (other than the K.K.G.) that orders from on high, meaning the heads of the Luftwaffe and of the Air Transport Ministry, leave no doubt that "matters of the battery take precedence over school matters." In short, it is made unmistakably clear that Air Force people adhered closely to Hitler's own credo of "a heroic youth," part of which is quoted in *Mit 15 an die Kanonen*: "I want young people to grow up so that they will frighten the world, a violent, dominant, cruel youth. . . . I do not want intellectual education. . . . Young people must learn . . . to conquer the fear of death—that is the standard of a heroic youth."

In Emunds' book, one sees at various times that the Luftwaffe men regarded *Flakhelfer* as pampered striplings, subjecting them to considerable harassment. Illustrating this, a *Flakhelfer* looks back with distaste on a sergeant who ordered him to remove a spiderweb with his face. The *Flakhelfer* says, "I thought to myself, If I ever meet that guy after the war, I'll beat his brains out." The same sort of hazing carried over to church attendance, which was looked upon as an unseemly escapade. The boys discovered this on the one Sunday they were permitted to worship, for on returning from early Mass, they found their quarters a shambles, their belongings scattered, their beds overturned, litter everywhere. No sooner had the boys beheld this scene than an officer materialized, stridently barking, "In one hour this room is to be spic-and-span!" Nor did the episode end there, as a *Flakhelfer*'s deposition attests: "The following day, I had to report to a higher command, where I was asked why we had gone to church. I was made to stand at attention for two hours, perspiration pouring down my face; I was standing in an overheated room. I was told that Catholicism and sol-diering were incompatible, like railroad tracks that ap-peared to converge but were actually parallel."

The boys were trained to operate anti-aircraft guns and to identify enemy planes, but, as might be expected, their duties included menial chores. They were not, however, the lowliest of the low. That distinction went to a contingent of captured Russians who were officially designated *Untermenschen*—"subhumans." Their heads shaved, their garb prisoner-of-war overalls, the slave laborers led an ostracized existence, living in barracks sealed off by barbed wire, forbidden to eat or talk with Germans. The segregation was based on Nazi doctrine. As Slavs, the Russians, like Jews, were held beneath contempt. Like all Germans, *Flakhelfer* were given to understand that the dividing line between themselves and the foreign labor force was "drawn in blood." One *Flakhelfer* states, "It was impressed on us that the Russians were not real humans beings but subhumans and that we, as members of 'the pure race of Teutons,' were not to mingle with them." In one instance, when *Flakhelfer* were suspected of doing just that, they had to engage in a marching drill for more than an hour while wearing gas masks; confinement to barracks and loss of leaves were other punishments with which the boys were threatened for unbending with subhumans.

Unlike the rest, Russians ate out of washbowls. Nights, no matter the weather, they stood on duty near gun emplacements while others, also awaiting air strikes, sat huddled in partly underground bunkers that were heated by stoves. Inevitably, though, there were lapses in the rules, for captor and captive had joint assignments to carry out and, at times, each other's lives to save. According to Emunds' book, the boys, whenever it was possible, sneaked the Russians into the heated bunkers for a while or slipped them scraps of food, in exchange for which the Soviet citizens made brooms with which *Flakhelfer* could sweep their barracks. Emunds' book speaks, too, of the coolness that the Russians showed in

12

the face of the bombs that their would-be saviors rained on Aachen. Asked by an inquisitive *Flakhelfer* what sustained them, Soviet laborers answered that it was faith in the Red Army's eventual triumph. The book records that the Russians were puzzling figures to the high-school boys. They couldn't see that the *Untermenschen* were so very different from them—except one, who was a math marvel and helped them out with their lessons. In the end, a *Flakhelfer* recalls, the boys rationalized their confusing observations by deciding that these particular Russians were "exceptions."

As we learn from the book, even in a wartime dictatorship German parents did not surrender their fifteen-year-olds to the military without protest. Some parents adopted stalling tactics before entrusting their sons to the Luftwaffe's ministrations. One mother prevailed on a doctor friend to say that her fifteen-year-old had a bad heart; excused from service, it is recorded, the son wept tears of shame. A *Flakhelfer* recalls a visit he made home when the fall of Aachen appeared imminent. He says, "Father hinted I should remain . . . but I considered it my duty to return. . . . I would have thought myself a coward. . . . He took me to the railroad station, expressing the hope that we would soon see one another again. Alas, I never again did see him or any other member of my family."

13

Parents weren't alone in their concern for the young draftees. A number of government officials opposed the conscription of adolescents, among them Martin Bormann and Hjalmar Schacht, two of Hitler's best-known collaborators. The particular fear that had grownups in Aachen and throughout Germany on edge was that the youngsters would be placed in "moral jeopardy" (*sittliche Gefährdung*) by being thrown in with rough types—woodsmen from the Bavarian Alps, for example—who would not hesitate to hold forth explicitly (*aufklären*) about the mysteries of sex. As it turned out, the qualms were warranted. One finds in the book that two *Flakhelfer,* one of them a *Mannschaftsführer,* or team leader, of his battery, witnessed the public seduction of one of their comrades by two prostitutes. The book carries two letters that support the fears of older people concerning the boys' tender sensibilities. In one of the letters, the commanding general of the Luftwaffe's Seventh District, which took in Aachen, writes, "According to reports from teachers, regular Luftwaffe personnel are trying to enlighten *Flakhelfer* in the ugliest manner about sexual matters. I hereby request that commanding officers make personal efforts to see to it that such incidents are henceforth prevented. . . ." The second letter went to the Reichsminister of Education in Berlin, its author an important Party official in Münster, who wrote, "Some soldiers who feel inferior to *Flakhelfer* think they can impress the youngsters by telling them dirty stories. . . . The boys are made to believe that it is unmanly not to engage in sexual intercourse. Thus, the danger exists that the boys will become wavering in their moral standards . . . and that they will lose their sense of decency and propriety."

14

This issue, though, like so many others, faded as the country's military fortunes declined; it was recognized on all sides that every bit of help was needed to stave off defeat. Enthusiasm for *der Führer,* once so vociferous, became muted as German forces fell back. The book puts it bluntly: "After the Allied invasion in June, 1944, the opinion of most *Flakhelfer* about the war varied at exactly the same rate at which Germany's situation deteriorated." Most notably, this manifested itself on July 20, 1944, when a ring of officers and aristocrats, numbering perhaps a thousand, were caught plotting Hitler's assassination. According to statements in the book, the boys wondered whether this development was good or bad—their very first show of political awareness. They found the news bewildering. They had been reared to believe in *der Führer's* infallibility since as far back as they could remember; the path of least resistance, as the book brings out, was to think of the plotters as "traitors" and ponder the matter no further. But there was an exception, a *Flakhelfer* named Horst. On hearing of the assassination attempt, Horst exclaimed, "Did they get the pig at last?" Several *Flakhelfer,* gathered in their barracks, were with him at the time, and when one of them disappeared abruptly, the others suspected he had left to turn in Horst. A buddy of Horst's chased after the imagined informer and found him standing outside, taking the air. He was indignant at the buddy's suspicions. "I heard nothing, absolutely nothing," he told Horst's pal. Politics, it appeared, had yet to undermine the unthinking bond of adolescence.

A far more important prod to the boys' political education than the July 20 *Attentat,* one learns, was the aerial pounding that Aachen took—the area afforded Allied crews a complex of juicy targets, including railroad yards, factories that turned out railroad cars and U-boat engines, and a network of ground defenses that the Allies wanted to soften up for their advancing troops. Gradually, as the raids continued without letup, *Flakhelfer* were increasingly drawn to accepting one of two attitudes toward the regime. One held that *der Führer* would yet deliver victory, the other that all was lost and that the only sensible course left was to save one's skin. Analyzing his loss of faith, a proponent of the latter view states, "If 2,000 aircraft can fly over the city unchallenged and we can't even bring down twenty percent of them, then something is wrong." By the summer of 1944, bribes for false air-raid alarms were a thing of the past, and so, pretty much, were the visits of teachers; hours that the boys had once put in for classes were now spent playing cards in wheat fields near the batteries. By then, one reads, with all public transport knocked out, parents trudged through the smoking city to see whether their offspring lived. Fifteen of them did not, and in each instance the parents were given two hundred *Reichsmark* for burial expenses. A *Flakhelfer* recalls running to hide when the parents of a friend who had just been killed arrived to visit their son. In a similar incident, a second *Flakhelfer* recalls how he handled matters in the face of yet another parental visit: "Herbert's parents stood at the

16

entrance looking for their son. I happened to be right there. I thought, Oh, my, how can I, a young boy who's still alive and healthy, be the one to tell them that their son is dead? All I could say was, 'Poor Herbert, he's not feeling so well.' "

By September, 1944, all was in a state of collapse. The Americans were about to enter Aachen, and an ex-major, one of three Luftwaffe officers interviewed in Emunds' book, recalls asking himself, "Why sacrifice young people unnecessarily?" Fifty *Flakhelfer* were with him at the time, and the major, though unauthorized to do so, took matters into his own hands. He had no idea whether the homes of any of them still stood, but he told the youngsters gathered around him, "Now, you boys, go home, go home!"

2   *A Tiny Flag*

In Aachen, I made my way to Emunds' house, a modest dwelling of yellow stucco, where I was greeted at the door by the teacher and his wife, a green-eyed, reddish-haired woman in her middle years; hospitably, she said tea would be ready for her husband and me when we had finished talking. Emunds showed me to his study, a small room with a large crucifix hanging above the doorway. He was of medium height, with a graying black mustache, and he smoked incessantly. He told me he had fought in Russia as an artilleryman and, along with thousands of other Nazi troops, had been taken prisoner in Bohemia, on the last day of the war; he had spent three years in Siberia. Emunds has three sons, the oldest of whom, Martin, was eighteen and about to graduate from the K.K.G. Out of curiosity, Martin, a tall, brown-haired boy sporting a semi-Afro, joined his father and me at the start of our talk. Emunds began by, again, expressing his surprise at the interest his classroom assignment had aroused, attributing it to the relatively small amount of German writing about the war. Much of what had appeared, he said, dealt with German resistance (*Widerstand*)—notably, the so-called Officers' Plot of July 20, 1944. Emunds said, "Some Germans still observe that date, but they have opposition—it's still a controversial matter." Martin shifted in his chair, his curiosity apparently spent. Emunds smiled wearily. "Our young people are all alike; they don't want to hear about the war," he told me. "They have Hitler on their minds about as much as they do Charlemagne."

I asked Martin whether that was so, and he replied, "I think of modern problems that have to do with now, with the future." Politely, he excused himself, saying he had to study for an exam.

Ten years earlier, Emunds remarked as he watched his son leave, it wasn't at all uncommon for children to tell off their parents for having backed a barbaric dictatorship that had invented extermination camps. Such scenes were infrequent now, but one still heard of them. Parents in particular, Emunds informed me, had welcomed the publication of *Mit 15 an die Kanonen,* many of them, it appeared, hoping to take on a certain stature in the eyes of their progeny. Pressing copies of the book into the hands of their children, they had urged them to read about the wartime pressures and dangers they had undergone, to persuade them that the comfortable lives they now took for granted had come in the wake of national suffering and sacrifice. Naturally, as a parent himself, Emunds hoped that *Mit 15 an die Kanonen* could bring that about, but, really, he asked, how was one to tell? All he had had in mind was to give his students a novel, stimulating assignment. A couple of moments later, though, on reflection, Emunds added another motive. As a history teacher, he said, he felt a certain obligation to pass on whatever firsthand information he could to future historians studying the dozen years that the Third Reich had lasted. He had worked as quickly as he could in compiling the material, he said, for even history that we ourselves make has a way of slipping past us, "like a flowing river." He had taught history for many years and was still uncertain as to its uses. He rejected Cicero's precept *"Historia magister vitae"* ("History is the teacher of life"), on the ground that it made too much of history. The most that history could do, he thought, was teach us how to avoid repetition of catastrophe. "Perhaps it can give us warnings," Emunds said. "I want to believe that, even though it may not be true. If I didn't, it would be very hard to go on being a history teacher."

Mrs. Emunds' tea proved to be a feast of varied delicacies, its principal ornament a small wheel of Camembert in whose exact center she had placed a tiny American flag. "In your honor," Mrs. Emunds said, bowing her head. We sat in the living room, she and Emunds and I; now and then, Martin and his two brothers darted in, long enough to help themselves to pastry. Mrs. Emunds seemed delighted when I told her I liked the Camembert; she seemed even more pleased when I expressed admiration for her home. She told me, "It was destroyed in the war. American planes did it." The original house, she went on, had belonged to her family; she had been raised in it. She had pictures of the demolished structure—did I care to see them? Before I could answer, she fetched them from a bureau, and I found myself leafing through a sheaf of faded snapshots. Mrs. Emunds stood over me, saying nothing. Holding the pictures in my hands put me in mind of the book's oft-repeated phrase "terror bombing." Mrs. Emunds did speak when I came to a snapshot that showed nothing but a shallow crater. Her tone even and pleasant, she said, "That was the cellar. My parents and two of my sisters and my brother were killed there." She and another sister had been away at the time, at school in Koblenz. After the war, the house had been rebuilt from the ground up.

When I gave the snapshots back she told me that Aachen had been the first German city taken, and I heard myself say that I was aware of that—that a friend of mine, an American, had been killed in its capture. "He's buried near here, in Belgium, in a military cemetery," I said.

There was a brief silence, which Emunds terminated. "When you wish, Martin and I will drive you there," he said. He looked at his son, who was gorging himself on cake. I hadn't expected to talk about my friend. I rose, and we shook hands all around, my first visit to the resurrected home at an end.

It's off to war we go!

Student soldiers—soldier students

Entrance to the Kaiser-Karls-Gymnasium

Flakhelfer Franz Josef
Emunds

At last—Paul Emunds and students present *Mit 15 an die Kanonen*

Downed aircraft

Fallen American

At his post

A Passing Phenomenon   3

The following day, I used a list that Emunds had drawn up and had given to me at his home. On it were the names of people he had found for me to interview; I was assured that none would be speaking anonymously—a departure from the approach employed in *Mit 15 an die Kanonen*. The first of these people whom I met with was Father Heinrich Selhorst, an elderly cleric who had taught religion at the K.K.G. and other schools in Nazi times. He had retired some years earlier and lived now with his sister, a lame, heavyset woman in her late seventies.

The two shared a dark, street-level apartment in one of several small houses reserved for priests, half a block away from the cathedral square. Thoughtfully, Emunds had one of his students, a strapping seventeen-year-old named Lorenz Trümper, guide me on the brief walk from the K.K.G., which I had been visiting, to Father Selhorst's apartment. The priest waved us both to chairs; his sister puttered in the kitchen. Lorenz, I noticed, took his place self-consciously, but soon, his eyes wide, he was listening raptly to Father Selhorst's words. They came easily. The priest, portly and gray-haired, his black raiment loose-fitting, was not only pleased at having the company of visitors but also, it turned out, eager to speak up for the good name of the Germans. Perhaps fittingly, he subscribed to the devil theory of history. Hitler, he asserted, had been a godless misleader of his countrymen. "They never believed in him, they considered him mad," Father Selhorst maintained. They had followed Hitler solely out of fear for their jobs, their families, their lives. Hitler had been a passing phenomenon. His like would never be seen again. Glancing at Lorenz, the priest said he was at a loss to understand why schoolboys were made to study Hitler—his name was not worthy of utterance. *"Damnatio memoriae et erasio nominis,"* Father Selhorst intoned.

24

Having set forth his point of view, the priest proceeded to elaborate on it. In Aachen and elsewhere, he said, he had seen for himself that the Germans were not behind Hitler. In Aachen, he told me, students at the K.K.G.

preferred to listen to him rather than to attend meetings of the Hitler Youth. The priest said, "At Hitler Youth meetings, the young were indoctrinated with the beliefs of Adolf Hitler. When I talked to small groups, it would be about the difference between a saint and a hero— between care for others and care for one's own glorification." Eventually, in 1939, a boxing instructor at the Hindenburg School in Aachen, a Nazi fanatic, reported Father Selhorst to the authorities, charging that he was undermining the morale of young people. Father Selhorst was sent to Dachau, and he spent three years there. He arrived in the company of a Jew, who, he learned, was soon executed by means of an intravenous injection of gasoline. Uneasily, Father Selhorst said, "That didn't happen to me." With other inmates, he was used as a farmhand; the camp administration augmented its budget by selling farm crops to the public. Occasionally, coming in from the fields, Father Selhorst carried the remains of cattle that had been accidentally butchered by British bombers; the meat was also sold. The camp paid for labor—at least, at the time Father Selhorst was there. The pay was paltry, but, even so, attempts were made to relieve the field workers and the others of their earnings. An outstanding instance of this, Father Selhorst recalled, was the establishment of a bordello. The project didn't succeed. The inmates didn't have the strength for sex— neither the women selected to serve as concubines nor the men who might have been customers. In the end, Father Selhorst said, the clergymen at the camp were punished for allegedly fomenting a boycott of the brothel. "We lost our bread rations for two weeks," Father Selhorst said. Three thousand clergymen, from more than two dozen countries, were at Dachau, their living quarters isolated from those of the other inmates, he said. The camp's overseers, the priest told me, kept close guard against the spread of religious doctrine. Father Selhorst said, *"Veritas et caritas*—truth and love—sustained me throughout those years. In Dachau, I became as much a human being as it has been given for me to be."

Moving with effort, the priest's sister entered the room; a kitchen appliance wasn't functioning, and she wanted his help. The two stood together a moment, their closeness palpable—in age, in looks, in their long and daily need of each other. When they left, Lorenz spoke in a hushed whisper. He was exhilarated. He told me, "He's the first person I've ever met who was actually in a camp. Up to now, I'd only *heard* about those places. When my mother was a little girl, her parents used to worry that her father might be sent to a camp. They told her never to tell anyone what she heard at home."

Father Selhorst came back in a few minutes, apparently having reminded himself that he had set out to prove that Hitler never truly won the support of the German people. He cited the behavior of some of the S.S. guards at Dachau. One of them, he said, had told him in so many words that it was wrong for someone like him to be imprisoned, because in no way did he have *"eine dunkle Existenz"* ("a dark existence")—living with something to hide, that is, such as having been a Communist or a criminal. And another S.S. man, unburdening himself, told the priest that he deplored the government's cruel treatment of the inmates. "Why don't you tell someone in Berlin?" Father Selhorst asked, and the guard replied, "How can I? We S.S. men are just little people. I would lose my job. I might be sent to the Russian front." Spelling out the guard's response for me, Father Selhorst said, "The guard, you see, was acting not out of admiration for Hitler but out of simple fear." Throughout his incarceration, the priest went on, he perceived signs of goodness among the guards. They came to him with worries about relatives back home; they asked him to write letters to brothers and cousins who were about to marry or to the bereaved parents of fallen friends. And, for their part, Father Selhorst said, the guards helped *him* with *his* correspondence—they got his messages out of the camp uncensored, and that was *verboten*. "I wrote to my sister eighty times, all about myself, all about the details of life at the camp," he told me. Nor, he added, was he unique. Plenty of other prisoners had messages smuggled to the outside world. And, the priest continued, his voice rising, if one multiplied Dachau by the number of other camps, then there must have been many, many messages that reached friends and relatives; and these people, in turn, must have passed on the contents to *their* friends and relatives, and this process, Father Selhorst concluded, had gone on for years and years. He fell silent, and when he spoke again, it was not to dispense praise. Why was it, he asked, that so many of his countrymen now denied having known, during the war, of the camps' existence, of the things that had gone on there? "When will this falsehood leave us?" Father Selhorst asked. "It is like a devil's curse—Hitler's curse. Aren't those times of long ago dark enough? Do we have to go on living with a lie?"

One of Father Selhorst's students at the K.K.G. had been Rolf Lantin, who was now himself a teacher at the school, and it was to his home that I drove after leaving the dim apartment near the cathedral square. Lantin lived, with his wife, in a small stucco house in Aachen, whose most striking feature, as far as I was concerned, was a steep, ladderlike staircase that one had to negotiate before attaining the teacher's study, which was where we talked. The room was small and strewn with books on history and German literature, the subjects that Lantin taught at the K.K.G. It was easy to see why Emunds had put Lantin's name on his list, for Lantin, I found, besides having been a *Flakhelfer,* was someone who needed no priming to recall the war. Its memory was very much with him, as he attested, and as one could tell from a stricken expression that occasionally invaded his frank brown eyes. He was pushing fifty but looked younger, his narrow face scarcely lined, his hair black and only just beginning to recede. His voice was gentle, and his first words had to do with *Mit 15 an die Kanonen.* Its publication, he hoped, would give young people some comprehension of the Nazi repression, of how difficult it had been "for Germans to behave decently." In Lantin's opinion, this had been especially difficult for heads of families, who had mouths to feed. He himself had been only eighteen when the war ended, so he could lay claim to no such excuse. Nevertheless, Lantin said, he had had his share of burdens. These had come his way after he completed his stint as a *Flakhelfer* and donned an Army uniform—with, as he put it, his shoulders squared and his heart beating for adventure. He had been a good soldier, Lantin said objectively, obeying orders, but not blindly. He had used his eyes, it appeared, and most assuredly he had done so on a certain freezing day in January of 1945, when he and three others had been on guard duty at the railroad station in Weimar, not far from the concentration camp at Buchenwald. It was on that day, Lantin said, that he saw camp inmates for the first time. Hundreds of them, organized in squads of eight, had passed before his startled gaze, each squad a work detail on its way to reconstruct bombed dwellings. But they hadn't just passed. "They ran!" Lantin exclaimed, a haunted look in his eyes. "It wasn't necessary, but they were being forced to run to their forced labor, and they were all skeletons, hundreds of them—unburied skeletons shrouded in striped uniforms." Later that day, Lantin and his three comrades had watched the inmates fighting like animals for scraps of bread that S.S. men tossed into their ranks. The feeding had made a repellent scene, Lantin said, but what had laid hold of him and the three other guards was the sight of the long, grisly procession, its members thinly clad against the frost, all of them panting, their puffs of breath curling in the winter air. That night, the four young soldiers had made a solemn pact that if ever they saw an inmate trying to escape, they would not shoot. Nothing had come of the pact, Lantin told me, but the image of the running cadavers had chased him down through the years, never letting him forget that he had seen with his own eyes that inmates of concentration camps did indeed exist, enslaved and degraded. Yes, he had had nightmares about it since, Lantin said ruefully, but he had experienced yet another consequence: his sense of beauty had been damaged, his enjoyment of art numbed. That might sound to some like a precious punishment, he said, but it was important to him, and he didn't see how he could fail to mention it. He quoted a line from a book by Theodor Adorno, a German musicologist and thinker: "To write poetry after Auschwitz is barbaric."

Like Emunds, Lantin thought that his country had produced surprisingly little writing about the Third Reich—though in the last few years, he added, there had been intimations that a change might be in the making. At any rate, Lantin continued, much of the writing that had come out advanced the proposition—which I had just heard from Father Selhorst—that it was Hitler from whom all villainies had flowed. Lantin found this unfortunate. It had the effect of exculpating Germans for having made the Third Reich possible; it undermined the idea of personal accountability. His taste of Nazism, Lantin went on, had affected his teaching. He was determined to inculcate a challenging, critical sense in his students—something that had been denied his own generation, he said, which had been slavish in its veneration of authority. Certainly, Lantin said, the Allies' "reeducation program," directly after the war, hadn't turned things around. It had been a conqueror's program, prepackaged and sloganized, but then, he said, nothing of an educational nature could have succeeded at that time. Bread and wood were then everyone's watchwords.

Lantin told me how the end of the war had come for him. He had been lying on the floor of a makeshift hospital in Berlin, having suffered a bullet wound in his left leg during the defense of the city. It was the first week of May, 1945, and Red Army soldiers had burst into the capital, angry victors taking their revenge however they pleased. Grabbing up clothes left behind by a departed civilian patient, Lantin had thrown away his military uniform and documents and passed himself off as Dutch, attributing his wound to American planes. Limping, he had set out for Aachen, four hundred miles away. He was eighteen, and he wanted to be home with his mother and father. He didn't know whether they were still alive or whether his home—the house we were sitting in—was still intact. His plight was commonplace; thousands of German soldiers were wandering the roads, homeward bound. En route, Lantin recalled, he encountered a Soviet soldier. Noticing a book bulging in Lantin's knapsack, the Russian had yanked it out, flinging it at Lantin's feet. Timorously, Lantin had said, "That's Goethe's *Faust*," whereupon the Russian, perhaps anticipating Adorno, ground the book under his heel. Lantin had pushed on, living from hand to mouth, swimming the Elbe one night, his good leg kicking him a half kilometer to the river's west bank. Chaos was everywhere, transportation and shelter a matter of wild chance. Lantin began to feel safe only when he reached Düsseldorf, which was well behind American and British lines. He had been on the road for nearly two months before he spied the familiar but now broken outlines of Aachen; its population, much of it evacuated or dead, had gone down from a hundred and sixty thousand to about forty thousand. After wending his way for hours through streets made surreal by rubble and ruins, Lantin finally came to his home; now his voice, which had been quiet, took on a buoyant quality. He said, "I cannot describe the joy that that moment brought me. My mother and father were alive, both of them, and the house stood." A moment later, as though Lantin were punishing himself, his exultation vanished. Soberly, he said he did not want me to think he regarded his family reunion as a happy ending to the war. His eyes perplexed, he said, "All that the war taught us was that we had to make a new beginning. We knew only what we did not know—how to be at peace, how to be young, how to think for ourselves. Perhaps we've learned those things, but I'm not sure. We still seem to respond to authoritarianism.

There are times when I think that—with different details, of course—the whole business could happen again. Dictatorship is possible in every age."

The day after I saw Lantin, I kept an appointment at the home of Leo Haupts, a former *Flakhelfer* who is now a professor of modern history at Cologne University, forty miles from Aachen, where he still lives; it was Haupts who wrote the introduction to *Mit 15 an die Kanonen,* in which he observed that the book enabled *Flakhelfer* to see themselves "involved with history . . . [and] without need . . . to portray themselves as heroes." Entering the Haupts' living room, which was tastefully furnished and pervaded by an atmosphere of settled harmony, I found myself cordially received by Haupts and his family: Mrs. Haupts, a wan blue-eyed woman with honey-blond hair; Stefan, fourteen; and Michael, seventeen, who had a struggling mustache of blond down. Stefan wasn't with us long. Like Emunds' son Martin, he decided that harking back to the Third Reich wasn't for him and soon took his leave. Michael, though, stayed on. An alert, intelligent young man, he had had a direct hand in the compilation of *Mit 15 an die Kanonen,* having served as one of the K.K.G. interviewers.

Attired in a navy-blue suit that set off a neatly knotted foulard and metal-rimmed glasses, Michael's father, a short, dark-haired man, talked of the Hitler years with an air of genial, genteel detachment. Touching on

Emunds' paperback, the professor said he was confident that it owed its popularity in large part to an interest of young people in the hardships that their parents had withstood. Michael differed at once; he spoke insistently, his tone dispelling the room's contented atmosphere. As far as he was concerned, he said, the book was nothing more than a nostalgic souvenir for oldsters. For him, Michael went on, the book had but a single use: it gave him information about the war. His parents and their friends rarely talked about it, and when they did it was to impress upon the young how soft a life they led. Michael said to me, "If your father tells you to clean up the garden and you don't feel like it, he says, 'Oh, if you only knew how hard we had it in the war!'" Well, Michael said, now he did know a little about those hard times, but he could not see what good they had accomplished. "I can imagine everything happening all over again," he said, echoing Lantin.

Mrs. Haupts appeared shocked. Apologetically, she said to me, "I can't understand my son."

Michael said, "We Germans are deeply proud of our economy and technology, but we try to hide our pride from other countries. We don't want them to think we could go back to our high-and-mighty ways." He read publications put out by Amnesty International, Michael informed me, and he knew for a fact that the use of violence was standard practice throughout the world; and *that,* he said emphatically, was not good—it could set old juices flowing in countries with militaristic pasts. "Patriotism," "the Fatherland," "the state"—such concepts, Michael said, were alien to his thinking. Next year, when he turned eighteen, he would have to choose between taking military training and performing *Ersatzdienst* ("alternative service"). Like several of his classmates at the K.K.G., he would be opting for *Ersatzdienst*.

Speaking hesitantly, Mrs. Haupts said, "In my youth, we didn't compare one political idea with another. We just wanted to be led, to have a leader."

"We were also idealistic," Professor Haupts reminded her. "We wanted to help our country. We had heard so much about unemployment and inflation—and, of course, there had been the defeat in 1918." Recalling the defeat that he himself had experienced in 1945, Haupts said that two or three years after that took place German moviegoers had laughed at Hitler when he was shown on the screen; five years later, however, they had stopped laughing. His genial detachment momentarily deserting him, Haupts said, "We can't forget what we did, but we can't explain it." On a recent vacation in England, Haupts said, he and his family discovered that the British, too, remembered Hitler, but did so openly. The family had been astonished to find an abundance of books, plays, and television programs dealing with the Third Reich; there had even been comic books that recounted the gallantry of the Royal Air Force in the Battle of Britain.

Mrs. Haupts said, "Our whole childhood was given over to Hitler. Parents had to be careful of how they acted with their children. One day, I remember, Mother came into my room when I was putting up a picture of Hitler, and she said, 'Oh, I know a better place to hang it—let's hang it on the kitchen wall.' We did, and soon the heat from the stove spoiled *der Führer's* face. Another time—I was nine or ten—Mother made me stand at the window and watch two policemen leading a group of Jews to the railroad station. The policemen were crying."

Haupts, too, had known of the deportation of Jews during the war, he told me, but that was all. He said he had known nothing about concentration camps. He didn't envy Germans who had, he said—they probably lived with a guilty conscience. I asked Michael whether any legacy of guilt had come down to young Germans, and he shook his head. "Why should it?" he demanded indignantly. "We weren't even born!" His spirited reply drew a nod of approval from his father, and the two exchanged a smile, their abjuration of guilt a bond between them. Mrs. Haupts watched them, relieved. His detachment back, Haupts said good-naturedly that he wondered whether concentration camps were destined to be remembered. In time, the professor observed, facts could turn fuzzy, lending themselves to revision. He cited an example. Among historians, he informed me, it had long been accepted that Charlemagne had decapitated four thousand Saxons in the eighth century for stealing cattle from the Franks. Well, Haupts said, in recent years some historians had been leaning toward the view that the Saxons had not been massacred but merely banished. Haupts concluded, "It's only speculation, of course, but it may be that there will come a day when people will ask, 'Were there really concentration camps, or was that just a myth?' "

Another *Flakhelfer*, Günter Frentz, had become a local newspaper reporter since the war, and his manner, I found, was much like that of many newspapermen I have met—brash, outspoken, pulling no punches. Frentz had a small house in Mausbach, a village east of Aachen, and we talked in his living room. He was bald and tall, his height accentuated by the room's low ceiling and by the fact that I was seated as he paced the floor, seemingly propelled by an eagerness to move his thoughts. First off, Frentz wanted me to know that he didn't think much of the general effect of *Mit 15 an die Kanonen*. It put him off, he said, the way other ex-*Flakhelfer* carried on about their suffering. They seemed to confuse it with idealism, and, Frentz asserted, there had certainly been none of that—unless one equated it with allegiance to the regime. Frentz said, "We were just youngsters, yes, but we were running with the pack—why not face it?" Continuing to pace restlessly, he told me that it irked him no end to find *Flakhelfer* in Emunds' paperback repeatedly claiming that it was only after the war that they learned to think. Forcefully, Frentz said, "It did *not* take the war to teach us the difference between right and wrong, between beauty and ugliness." Even before he was a *Flakhelfer*, he had begun to "think," if that meant sensing that Nazi

37

ideology wasn't all there was to life, if it meant recognizing that there was a transcendent human spirit—*ein Geist*. Immersing himself in the verse of Heinrich Heine had awakened him to this consciousness, Frentz told me; and he added that the great poet, a Jew, was on a long list of proscribed writers. Frentz laughed dryly. American soldiers had captured him in the spring of 1945, he recalled, and their anti-Semitic mouthings as they marched him to an interrogation center would have warmed the cockles of Hitler's heart.

Frentz returned to *Mit 15 an die Kanonen,* laying about him with easy ferocity at the book's contents. It would have been nice, he said, if it had touched in the slightest on the truckling deportment of school administrators during the Hitler era. Specifically, Frentz said, he had in mind the K.K.G., his alma mater. Whenever suspicions of being anti-regime hovered over the school, as they did over all schools, the headmaster would advise security officials to investigate the parents, not the faculty. In retrospect, Frentz remarked sardonically, it had been good advice, for, with rare exceptions, the teachers at the school had been a collection of prudent party-liners. "Would you like their names?" Frentz asked me. When I declined his offer, he looked disappointed for a moment, then gave his attention to the Catholic Church, of which he was a member. According to him, nowhere in *Mit 15 an die Kanonen* could one find a breath of criticism concerning the Church's actions, even though everyone knew that the hierarchy had been as pro-Hitler as the leaders of any Protestant denomination. Nowadays,

Frentz said, it was fashionable among Catholics to blame Prussians and Protestants for the Nazis' accession to power, but hadn't Bavaria, a Catholic stronghold, been the birthplace of the Nazi movement? And what was so great about his own bailiwick, the Rhineland? It, too, was predominantly Catholic, and it hadn't exactly served as a bastion of anti-Nazism.

"What about Father Selhorst?" I inquired, and, grudgingly, Frentz replied, "He admired aristocrats, but he did have courage. He wasn't like most priests."

"Is it true that Germans don't care to remember the Third Reich?" I asked.

Frentz nodded, then recited an old German saying to the effect that the less Germans talk about something, the deeper their awareness of it is. He wasn't certain, Frentz went on to say, but conceivably a measure of contrition had something to do with this reluctance to recall the Third Reich. The treatment of the Jews, he said, had been a phenomenal, a unique cruelty; he estimated that nine out of ten of the death-camp inmates had been Jews, though Jews had made up less than one percent of Germany's population and less then ten percent of the population of the Nazi-occupied countries.

Did he think all wars produced their horrors, I asked. What about Hiroshima? What about Vietnam?

Frentz took no time to ponder his answer. "Hitler wasn't war," he said flatly, halting his pacing. He stared down at me and then, shaking his head, he said, "War is one thing, Hitler was another. No, no, they are not the same. Alibis are not for me."

4 Acres of Lawn

I was in Belgium, three or four kilometers from the village of Henri-Chapelle, having crossed a corner of the Netherlands to get there. Twenty minutes earlier, I had been in downtown Aachen, waiting outside my hotel for Emunds and his son Martin, who were making good their offer to drive me out to the American cemetery where my friend was buried. After attending Sunday Mass, the two had picked me up in a run-down family car, and, with Martin at the wheel, we had got under way; Emunds had brought a camera. The cemetery was situated in terrain over which once-famous battles had been fought—Bastogne, Malmédy, and others, all part of the Battle of the Bulge. The weather was drizzly, and when we had parked the car we took shelter awhile under the flat roof of a stone colonnade whose pillars were inscribed with the names of nearly five hundred men listed as missing in action. Before us were those whose bodies had been recovered—eight thousand in all, ninety-four of them unknown—their markers spread over an immense acreage of lawn running on toward a flagstaff from which hung an American standard. I didn't know where to look for my friend's grave, and, obligingly, Emunds and Martin went off to find someone who did. Alone in the colonnade, which sat on a knoll, I had a sweeping view of the countryside, rolling and peaceful, whose far reaches, I had learned, took in other military cemeteries, American, French, British, some of them more populous than the one I was gazing at. Only the living relieved the wet, cheerless scene. Wearing bright-colored raincoats, a party of fifteen girls had gathered near a grave perhaps two hundred yards from where I stood; the girls, ten or twelve years old, were in the charge of a nun, who was lecturing. Near the group, an elderly couple, their hands entwined, peered at a succession of headstones, plainly searching for a particular name. Apart from these old and young people, stillness reigned over the vast expanse of crosses and Stars of David. I had never been to a military cemetery before, and seeing this one took me aback. Unlike a churchyard, it had no lichened, half-collapsed graves.

41

Here the thousands of monuments that met the eye were severely alike in age and size, all stamped from identical white stone, all arrayed in rows of relentless symmetry, as though the interred dared not break ranks. The interred themselves, I thought, had had little to do with their fates: gigantic events and the judgments of strangers, friendly and unfriendly, had contrived their demise. In a military cemetery, as nowhere else, it seemed to me, one could see with dazzling clarity the captivity in which imperial, impersonal forces could hold our lives; at Henri-Chapelle, the stony panorama could stir anew a yearning to lead a life of one's own, private and unassailed.

Drawn to the buried battalions, I left the colonnade, moving down a grassy slope that led to the cemetery proper. I had taken only a few steps when, directly behind me, someone said, "That's U.S. territory out there." The voice, I discovered, belonged to an American, an official of the American Battle Monuments Commission. Emunds and Martin were at his side, both pleased at having been able to find him on a Sunday. "He knows your friend's address," Emunds said. The official, it turned out, was a retired Army warrant officer from the Midwest who had stayed on in Europe. He spoke in a careful monotone, plying me with varied information. As the four of us descended the slope, which was lined by hedges, he said that the cemetery was fifty-seven acres in area and represented a gift of the Belgian government to America. The daily average of visitors was fifteen hundred; on holidays, such as Memorial Day, thousands came, including Germans, some of whom wept. A German, the official said, had once told him, "The war would have been different if we Germans had known how far in front of us your bullets were. We knew only that our own were right at our backs."

I moved away. I hadn't come to Henri-Chapelle to ponder any tangle of German motives. Seeing my friend's grave wasn't the sole reason I was in Belgium. Since arriving in Aachen, I had acquired a fresh incentive for making my visit: I hoped that it would restore to me the cleansing, simplifying anger I had known in the war, when right and wrong had been readily distinguishable, when treating with enemy explanations had been off limits. But time had spent the anger, and it would not come. Other things did, such as Emunds' picture-taking. When we reached my friend's grave, the American official retreated several yards, and Emunds, sizing up the day's light, went to work. My friend's tomb was a cross on which were inscribed his name, his status of war correspondent, and the exact date of his death, in 1944. He had been twenty-five and already a writer of solid reputation. Deliberately, I recalled topics we had talked about—jazz, girls, sports; absurdly, a track-and-field meet we had been to came back to me in a profusion of detail. Finally focussing his camera, Emunds called out for me to stand closer to my friend's tomb, but I paid no attention. My thoughts were with the hosts of dead around us. In my mind, they had arisen and were young again, as in 1944, and on their way to a front, ascending

43

winding mountain roads aswirl with dust from tramping feet, jeeps, half-tracks, open-hatched tanks. And again, as I had often seen them do, the climbers affected a lightheartedness, even though they knew full well that they would soon be taking casualties. It had been a necessary lightheartedness, sustaining in all a sense of immortality: others might die but not oneself. Those now at Henri-Chapelle had learned differently, but it didn't follow that any of their survivors—military or civilian, American or German—had given up the illusion that they themselves would go on forever. Only the suspension of time itself could persuade them to suspend that illusion. Until then, everything that happened—history—was but a forerunner of something else. Time ground all that befell us into incidents, discrete and transient, each fading in memory. Were we condemned to think of Hitler's deeds as but a passing incident? How could one keep from doing that? His camera still raised, Emunds shouted through the drizzle, *"Bitte, bitte,* move closer to your friend! To the stone—closer, closer!"*

For service to the
Fatherland

Sweeping the skies

Flakhelfer at ease

Kammeradschaft

Father Heinrich Selhorst,
priest and teacher

Ex-flakhelfer Gunter
Frentz: "Alibis are
not for me"

Mr. and Mrs. Paul
Emunds

Rolf Lantin—
nightmares and
memories

Jewish home in Berlin

Monument to atonement—Kissena Apartments in Queens

A city divided

Checkpoint Charlie

Belgium: at Henri St. Chapelle

"Where Were the Camps?" 5

The day before I left Aachen, I saw Pastor Heinrich Fuchs, of the Lutheran church in Heinsberg, a town a half hour's drive from the city. Unlike the other people I had met, Pastor Fuchs was not from the Rhineland—nor, for that matter, were his parishioners. They came from Prussia and Silesia, their numbers composed of *Vertriebene*—literally, "driven ones," meaning displaced persons who were forced from their homes by the Russians and Poles. In terms of *Mit 15 an die Kanonen*, Pastor Fuchs enjoyed a certain distinction. He had been a Luftwaffe officer, one of three whom Emunds had been able to locate. As though to demonstrate that he had been an officer, Pastor Fuchs had two of his former *Flakhelfer* on hand in the living room of his rectory, which was our meeting place. One of them was a cousin of Paul Emunds', named Franz Josef Emunds. He was a livestock farmer from nearby, moon-faced and apple-cheeked; his visage seemed to invite the outdoors into the large, immaculate room in which we sat, its décor heavy with settees and carved wooden chairs. The other ex-*Flakhelfer* was Ludovikus Oidtmann, a lively, dark-haired maker of church windows, who had been to America numerous times on business. Oidtmann spoke more than his farmer friend did. It was the pastor himself, though, who held forth at greatest length. Perhaps out of a continuing deference to his wartime officership, the two younger men, like adjutants, eyed him a moment before they themselves spoke. The pastor, gray-haired and of medium height, talked with an easy assurance and a steady smile. He had on glasses that glinted now and then, when the day's sunlight struck; he was wearing a blue suit and a maroon turtleneck. The pastor was married, as I learned when he said, regretfully, that his wife was away or she would have prepared us all a splendid meal.

46 By his own appraisal, Pastor Fuchs said, he had been a mature man of thirty in 1944, when he was assigned as a lieutenant to the Rhineland for anti-aircraft duty. By then, he went on, it was apparent that Germany's military fortunes were on the wane. Why else, he asked, would

the Luftwaffe have drafted children? As both Oidtmann and Franz Josef Emunds nodded in agreement, he said, "They were homesick, even though they were near home. I often let them go home without official permission. I tried to be like a father to them. I called them by nicknames."

"Mine was Bib," Oidtmann put in.

"Jo-Jo," Emunds said.

Such informality, the pastor wanted me to know, was highly irregular for an officer. If his superiors had found out about it, he said, they would have suspected his theological training, given the Luftwaffe's anticlerical outlook. It was only as a sop to churchgoers, Pastor Fuchs told me, that that branch of the German military had recruited divinity students like him, enticing them with good posts. He himself, the pastor granted, had managed well throughout the war and ever since—his congregation of *Vertriebene* were an admirable folk, industrious and thriving. Most of his compatriots at divinity school, however, had not fared so well; more than half had been killed. Continuing, he said he had been lucky to survive the heavy air raids in the Aachen area. In one of them, in the spring of 1944, he recalled, British Marauders, clobbering some railroad repair shops, had left a *Flakhelfer* dead. Shocked and distraught, the other fifteen-year-olds had been unable to look at the corpse. Lieutenant Fuchs had dismissed them for the day. "But a few hours later, without being asked, they came back, one by one, ready for duty," he went on, his steady smile now broad and pronounced. He and Emunds and Oidtmann looked at each other, pride on their faces.

Abruptly, Emunds' cherubic countenance clouded. His tone censorious, he said that he had presented copies of *Mit 15 an die Kanonen* to nephews of his but that their reactions had not been satisfactory; after reading the book, they had informed their uncle that they considered him an accessory to the Nazi cause, and that they themselves would not have served as *Flakhelfer*. The farmer said, "I told them that they would have done *exactly* as I had—maybe more so. I told them that they could not even have entered shool if they had not joined the Hitler Youth."

Oidtmann had undergone a similar experience. Watching a television program one evening, he had heard a K.K.G. student, one of those who had contributed to *Mit 15 an die Kanonen*, find fault with the manner in which his parents comported themselves during the war; the student had referred to concentration camps in a way that incensed Oidtmann. He said to me, "The boy talked as if the regime did not have absolute control over everything we read and heard. He talked as if we knew all about the camps and the gassing."

"What would you have done if you had?" I asked.

Deferentially, Oidtmann and Emunds waited for Pastor Fuchs to respond, and he did so unhesitatingly. "What *could* an individual have done?" he replied. "The Nazis had a complete spy system. Children reported their parents. When I gave sermons, I was warned to watch my words."

"Even the Pope was silent," said Oidtmann, a Catholic.

Emunds, also a Catholic, echoed Father Selhorst's view. "Hitler was like the Devil himself," he said.

Such times as the Third Reich had brought about would never return, Pastor Fuchs predicted. All was changed. The old chauvinism was dead; it would be a distant day indeed before the old martial tunes were heard again. Humorously, the pastor declaimed a couplet from one of them: " *'Wer für Deutschland gab sein Blut, Ruht in fremder Erde gut'* " ("He who gave his blood for Germany, Rests well in foreign soil").

Oidtmann, who was the father of four teen-agers, was still incensed by the television program he had watched. The young today, he said, hadn't the vaguest comprehension of how self-indulgent their lives were. He said, 'We didn't even know we were young. We skipped the years between childhood and manhood. One day I was a schoolboy and the next a *Flakhelfer*. And then one day I was a *Flakhelfer* and the next I was taking an oath as a member of the Army." He spoke intensely, as though his memories were a day old. He had fought with an armored division, eventually ending up in a prisoner-of-war camp in Belgium. "I was seventeen when I came back to Germany," he said "I wanted cigarettes that day, so I went to a tobacconist. He asked me my age, and when he heard it, he said, 'You have one more year to wait.' I couldn't believe my ears. I had dodged bombs, I had seen dead and wounded, I had been a prisoner of war, but a few cigarettes—that was *verboten, ganz verboten.*"

Pastor Fuchs spoke. Gravely, he gave it as his judgment

that his two underlings of long ago had aired sentiments with which he was inclined to agree. Yes, he said, the modern young did appear to be a different breed from Oidtmann's and Emunds' generation. "When you two were *Flakhelfer*, there was a feeling for others," he said to them. "We didn't even think about it, it was so natural. There was no selfishness, no one was egocentric, like now. In those days, we gave everything for the nation, we lived for something greater than ourselves."

My last hour in Aachen was spent in a classroom of fifteen-year-olds at the K.K.G. Twenty-two of them were taking a history course conducted in English. As I had learned in advance from Paul Emunds, the class had just reached a point in its semester where it was considering the Third Reich. Emunds had also told me that the classroom was in an old wing of the building, which had escaped the destruction visited on other parts of the school; *Flakhelfer* had once studied in the room we were occupying. Emunds was present as a history teacher, but the actual supervision of the class fell to Wilhelm Hellmann, a brown-haired teacher of English, about forty years old, who took great care to enunciate the foreign language slowly and clearly for the benefit of his students. They responded imitatively, so that their exchanges with Hellman gradually took on a metronomic quality. The class members looked much younger than Michael Haupts and the other seventeen-year-olds I had met—those who had helped put together *Mit 15 an die Kanonen*. The boys were dressed as one might expect—in jeans, scuffed shoes, tieless shirts. I had found as inconspicuous a place as I could in the rear of the room, but, inevitably, many of the boys eyed me as they took their seats. To explain my presence, Hellmann, after calling the class to order, announced that they had a visitor from America, and this elicited a fresh wave of head-turning. The students then faced the front of the room, where a screen had been lowered. Emunds prepared to give a slide-and-tape presentation, using equipment near my seat. The room was darkened, and he showed about two dozen slides, which included shots of Jews in the Warsaw ghetto; Storm Troopers in 1934 blocking patrons from entering Jewish-owned shops; anti-Nazis campaigning in the country's general election in 1932; Hindenburg shaking hands with Hitler, the victorious candidate, in 1933. The accompanying sound track was brisk and objective.

When the last slides had been shown, Hellmann switched on the lights and began to ask questions based on previous lectures and on homework as well as on the day's slides. His diction measured and orotund, he inquired of the class, "When we think of the Third Reich, what ideas come to mind?"

Hands shot up, and Hellmann pointed to a boy in a purple shirt, who replied, in fairly unaccented English, "When we think of the Third Reich, we remember that we lost the war and that Jews were murdered."

Hellmann went on to another question. "In olden days, there were holy wars," he said. "Was this a holy war?"

One boy raised his hand instantly, well ahead of three or four rivals, and Hellmann nodded at him. Eagerly, the boy said, "We had a crazy man who wanted the whole world."

"Hitler hypnotized the German people," another boy said.

"He knew Germans like very much discipline and militarism."

A stringbean of a boy said, "He gave employment, and he wanted to get land for *Lebensraum.*"

"Did Germany need living space?" Hellmann asked, translating the stringbean's German word.

There was much raising of hands, and a husky student with a breaking voice responded, "Germany lost land in the First World War and wanted to get it back."

Hellmann pointed a finger at a boy who was waving a hand desperately. "Germany needed room for markets and industry!" the boy shouted. He looked around him triumphantly.

"In the Caucasus Moutains, it gave much raw materials," a towheaded boy recited, the cadence of his English extremely slow.

"Yes, Tillmann," Hellmann said, indicating a boy in a checked shirt.

Tillmann said, "Germans thought that they were the best race in Europe. Germans thought that they had the duty to rule other nations."

Seeing that no other hands were raised, Hellmann took up the topic of oppression.

"Hitler oppressed the Jews," a paunchy student with thick glasses declared.

"Also oppressed were the opponents of the Third Reich," Tillmann said. "Old people were transported and were not seen again."

"Where were the camps?" Hellmann inquired.

"Mostly, the camps were in Bavaria and the camps were in Poland."

Hellmann said, "The camps were in places that were not so populated. Hitler did not wish the population to know about them. The German people were not able to have information."

At no other point did Hellmann volunteer commentary of his own. Immediately, he reverted to throwing out questions and getting back answers. Half the time, I found myself listening as much for the rhythm of the exchanges as for their substance. Pure and often high-pitched, the boys' voices reminded me that *Flakhelfer* had sat in the same room, no doubt answering questions about the First World War. Almost tangibly, dust seemed to be settling on events that would always be a part of my life; it was as though they were being torn from me— from my generation—and converted into mere history, remote and receding.

The last two answers I heard had to do with the future; "It cannot happen again unless it gives a Communist dictatorship." Another said, "We have a democracy. We know more than did our parents."

After that, a bell rang and the session came to an end, the boys noisily scraping their chairs against the floor as they shuffled to their feet.

6 *Quantified Atonement*

From Aachen, I went to Bonn, the seat of the Federal Republic of Germany. I wanted to talk with an official who could give me a backward look of a sort that was more encompassing in scope than the individual accounts I had been listening to. With the help of the foreign-press office, I was referred to Wolfgang Kaphammel, of the Ministry of Finance, who was in charge of the government's program of *Wiedergutmachung*, or restitution, the purpose of which was to make financial amends to, in the government's language, "the victims of Nazism." (*Wiedergutmachung* means making something good again.)

Correct and obliging, Kaphammel, a gray-haired man who wore gold-rimmed glasses, received me in his office, a neatly appointed room in a modern building at the intersection of Kennedy Allee and Martin-Luther-King-Strasse. Studiously, Kaphammel limited his remarks to *Wiedergutmachung* activities, which, I learned, derived from edicts issued by Germany's three Western conquerors—the United States, Britain, and France. (East Germany, in the Russian-occupied zone, pays some pensions to Nazi victims, but only if they are residents of East Germany. These payments are not called *Wiedergutmachung*, because the East German government maintains that it bears no responsibility for Nazi persecution.) Despite the foreign origin of the program, Kaphammel assured me, it had been carried out with a willing spirit. Indeed, he added, even before its inception, in the early fifties, the West German government, formed in 1949, had been restitution-minded; to support this claim, he produced an excerpt from a speech given in September, 1951, by West Germany's first Chancellor, Dr. Konrad Adenauer. Addressing the Bundestag, the Chancellor, a Catholic jailed twice by the Nazis, had stated, "In the name of the whole German people . . . unspeakable crimes have been committed and they demand restitution, both moral and material, for the persons and properties of the Jews who have been so seriously harmed."

Kaphammel went on to tell me that since those words

were delivered, West Germany has spent fifty-five billion marks (about twenty-five billion dollars at today's rate of exchange) on *Wiedergutmachung*, more than ninety percent of which has gone to Jews. The terms of restitution were worked out by West Germany, Israel, and the Conference on Jewish Material Claims Against Germany, which represents twenty-four Jewish organizations around the world. It took the better part of a decade to develop a reparations system, and at that it was an imprecise one, since, as Kaphammel suggested, there was no way of making it up to the Jews, Gypsies, and other claimants for every kind of loss that they might have undergone. How could amends be made for the simple act of having existed under Nazi rule? What adequate accounting could there be for the extermination of parents, the disappearance of whole communities, the sacking of synagogues? Professor Raul Hilberg, of the University of Vermont, author of *The Destruction of European Jews*, has compared efforts at *Wiedergutmachung* to a salvaging operation, its dimensions fixed by the "incompleteness" of Nazi destruction.

From the outset, in the early nineteen-fifties, Kaphammel said, it was apparent that the negotiations preceding the *Wiedergutmachung* program comprised no ordinary transaction. Indeed, extraordinary expectations attached to it, for in keeping with Chancellor Adenauer's conception, it was looked upon as the payment of a moral debt. In practice, though, the negotiating process among West Germany, Israel, and the Conference on Jewish Material

Claims Against Germany soon caused such lofty notions to lose altitude. West Germany's economy at the time was anything but prosperous, and its delegates, carrying out their mission efficiently, were ever mindful of that fact. In short, West German negotiators bargained hard, and the finished program shows it. Conditions adhere to its every provision. Thus, to cite a few examples, maximum limits, or ceilings, were imposed on all sections of the program, among them those dealing with loss of insurance payments, private pensions, and real-estate holdings. It was also stipulated that no restitution was to be paid for property lost outside Germany's 1937 borders, thereby foreclosing the possible claims of many thousands of victims who, after 1937, suffered losses of various sorts in France, Poland, and other Nazi-occupied lands. Nor could "persecutees"—those who did qualify for *Wiedergutmachung*—enter claims for property that was worth less than five hundred Reichsmark (approximately two hundred dollars) at the time of its loss. Such restrictions notwithstanding, West Germany's *Wiedergutmachung* program, as Jewish leaders readily grant, is a far more generous affair than anything to be found in the countries that fell under Russian dominion after the Nazi defeat. In fact, I was told, restitution programs of any scope have been unknown in that part of Europe, the explanation for which dates back to the Soviet Union's attitude in its hour of conquest—namely, that whatever was captured from the Nazis amounted to war spoils, pure and simple, for the victors to do with as they pleased. In the resulting nationalizing, and reconfiscating, that took place, refugees from Russian-controlled territory lost out on ever regaining shops, factories, farming acreage, and other assets. In a few isolated cases, governments in the Soviet sphere have made token contributions to resident Jews, now minuscule in number. Some of the contributions would appear to have been made almost capriciously. Shortly after the war, Rumania presented a collection of old furs to a national Jewish organization, and Czechoslovakia made the Jewish community of Bohemia-Moravia a gift of the abandoned concentration camp at Theresienstadt.

Kaphammel said that Israel has been among West Germany's beneficiaries, informing me that some eight hundred and fifteen million dollars' worth of goods and services were earmarked to go to the Jewish state over a twelve-year period, beginning in 1952. The credit, he said, was used for the acquisition of such basic needs as chemicals, heavy machinery, rolling stock for railroads, and merchantmen that were built in German shipyards. Hundreds of thousands of Jews who had been persecuted were seeking a homeland in the Middle East, and their influx, Kaphammel said, created enormous financial burdens for the infant nation. Israelis recoiled at the prospect of coming into German reparations and set up the cry of "Blood Money!" Tanks were called out to surround the Knesset building, so that debate on the issue could be conducted in relative calm. In the Knesset itself, many members shared the popular distaste for dealing with

Germans. In the end, though, Israel's dire straits persuaded a bare majority of the legislators to vote their consent. Israeli feelings, however, were soon exacerbated when German negotiators, doing their job, challenged Jewish requests by trimming estimates of the new state's needs, questioning the needs themselves, and suggesting that the influx of Jews from Eastern Europe might well be attributable to Communist rather than to Nazi actions. Negotiations were broken off at one point, and when they finally did culminate in agremeent, the Israeli Cabinet took no chances: impatient to get on with building a homeland, it bypassed the Knesset, refraining from asking for approval.

From Kaphammel, I learned that by the beginning of 1978 more than a million individuals, in quest of *Wiedergutmachung*, had filed almost four and a half million claims, two thirds of them originating outside West Germany. Principally, the claims have had to do with the loss of a family member's life; the loss of the claimant's own health; damage to property; and interference with the pursuit of the claimant's career. To offset inflation, Kaphammel said, the government has been augmenting its payments annually with cost-of-living adjustments. In determining reparations, I was told, Kaphammel's office has relied heavily for information on official records of the Third Reich, which turned out to be voluminous and self-incriminating; miraculously, the bulk of them escaped destruction during the war. Nazi archives at the Ministry of Finance and at the Reichsbank have yielded substantial data, which are open to the public and are so comprehensive that, I was told, in combing them many heirs of those eligible for *Wiedergutmachung* discovered holdings of which they had not been aware, such as utility shares or treasury bonds purchased long before Hitler came to power. In some instances, the files of internment centers, notably the one at Theresienstadt, turned up meticulously detailed inventories of property taken from inmates. Here, for example, is a partial list, with values, of the worldly goods of Frau Ansbacher, a widow who left for Theresienstadt on September 23, 1942:

Chest of drawers	Reichsmark 10
Kitchen table	5
Washstand	3.50
Bench	5
2 easy chairs	6
Bedstead	15
Brushwood kindling	7.5
Sofa	5
Desk	20
Bamboo chairs	10
Stove and pots	44
Coverlet	5

Before their deportation to the ghetto in Czechoslovakia, all inmates had to fill out forms (*Heimeinkaufsverträge*, "Home Purchase Contracts") containing more than two hundred queries designed to elicit a disclosure of one's total property. Apprised though they were that completion of the forms would mean automatic confiscation of that property, those bound for Theresienstadt answered the queries unhesitatingly, the reason being that the camp was played up throughout Germany as a model "old people's ghetto" (*Altersghetto*) to which only the truly fortunate among deportees could aspire; in exchange for their property, so the regime's promises went, applicants could look forward to spending their sunset years in safety and serenity. (Theresienstadt was a way station to Auschwitz, nearby.) Judging by a captured document, the process of expropriation was under way well before deportees entrained for the eastward journey. The document is a memo sent July 15, 1942, to the Police President of Aachen by a local representative of the Ministry of Finance, the agency responsible for property left behind in vacated apartments. In ten days, the Ministry official advises the Police President, "the last remaining Jews ... will probably be moved to Theresienstadt ... [and] everything must be done to avoid the possibility that unauthorized ... persons lay their hands on movable belongings of the Jews before I can take over." Requesting that police "watch the Jewish apartments several days in advance [of the impending deportations]," the Ministry official then supplies addresses of apartments about to be vacated—Eupenerstrasse 249, Promenadenstrasse 21, Königstrasse 22, Frankenbergerstrasse 20, all streets whose names I could recall having noticed without interest when I was in Aachen.

Documents by the ton came to light as a result of the Allied sweep through Germany, the invaders coming upon them in government buildings, warehouses, and salt mines—documents that included correspondence, military orders, minutes taken down at conferences, appraisals of enemy propaganda. The miscellany of captured information is as endless in variety as in quantity. One may find a note, for instance, that a prison warden at Minsk sent on May 31, 1943, to the General Commissar for White Ruthenia: "Since 13 April 1943, 516 German and Russian Jews have been finished off. . . . About 50 percent of the Jews had gold teeth, bridgework or fillings." Elsewhere, one reads that the gold was sent for melting to the Prussian State Mint. And other documents inform us that, for all the regime's anti-clericalism, Germans made much of Christmas. It was a season, it appears, for the distribution of "gifts" taken from those who had been exterminated, a ritual described as "utilization of the property of Jewish thieves." Nazi welfare organizations dispensed these mementos of Auschwitz and similar camps to deserving Germans. A welfare official, his mind fixed on the approaching yuletide of 1943, says, in writing to Heinrich Himmler, Reichsführer of the S.S., "Many a wounded [S.S.] man who does not own a watch or fountain pen would enjoy such a gift." The regime's largess, it is recorded, included men's and women's underwear, children's clothes, mechanical pencils, belts, suitcases, wallets, hats. It was no easy job, one also learns, preparing the presents for Christmas morn.

Many of the articles had to be repaired and polished. Watches had to be graded, the best going to soldiers of outstanding valor. Clothing was a trial: yellow Stars of David sewn to coats and dresses had to be detached; linings of garments had to be searched for valuables that might have been concealed. Laundering and fumigation were other things to think about, and at Kulmhof, an extermination camp in Poland, such chores were regarded as "hazardous duty"; personnel there were given extra pay for running the risk of "infection."

Paradoxically, the availability of abundant data has hindered as well as helped Kaphammel in dealing with the claims of survivors, for if nothing else many of the captured documents demonstrate that in numerous instances it is just about impossible to ascertain who is owed how much for what. The underlying reason for this, as already implied, derives from the plundering that was endemic to the Third Reich. It was a studied tack on the part of Nazi leaders, but such was its profligacy that even they, its sponsors, could not keep track of the pillage. At least one document bears this out—the minutes of a high-level meeting held in Berlin under the chairmanship of Hermann Göring, Reichsminister of the Luftwaffe and Germany's second-ranking Nazi; also present were Dr. Josef Goebbels, Minister for Propaganda and National Enlightenment; Reinhard Heydrich, Security Police Chief; and Kurt Daluege, Deputy Protector of Bohemia-Moravia. The conference took place at the Air Ministry on the morning of November 12, 1938—barely hours after the two-day rampage known as *Kristallnacht* (literally, Glass Night), in which mobs, organized and incited by the government, smashed the plate-glass windows of Jewish-owned shops and then, gathering momentum of their own, went on to kill any protesters and to set fire to synagogues. It was glass-smashing, though, that was at the heart of the rampage, and here the minutes record that something went wrong: too much glass was broken *Kristallnacht.* An insurance expert by the name of Hilgard is on hand to say so. Addressing Göring, he states that "the people" damaged so much glass that it will take manufacturers a half year to replace it.

GÖRING: The people will have to be enlightened on this.

GOEBBELS: We cannot do this right now.

GÖRING: This cannot continue! We won't be able to last with all this . . . [to Hilgard] Go on—you suggest, then, that the Aryan is the one who suffers the damage, is that right?

HILGARD: Yes . . . as far as glass insurance goes.

With display windows in smithereens, Germans everywhere made off with merchandise, which, it appears from the minutes, incenses the conferees. As devout Nazis, they feel that the pilfered goods belong to the State, not to anonymous freebooters. Here Hilgard speaks again, giving it as his opinion that the missing property has very likely vanished into the mists of untraceability. To support his view, he tells of what befell a Berlin jewelry store, located on the fashionable Unter den Linden.

64

HILGARD: The most remarkable of these [looting] incidents is the case of Margraf Unter den Linden. The jewelry store of Margraf is insured with us through a so-called combined policy that covers practically any damage that may occur. The store was completely stripped, and the damage reported to us amounted to 1,700,000 Reichsmark.

GÖRING: Daluege and Heydrich, you'll have to get me this jewelry through raids, staged on a tremendous scale . . .

DALUEGE (interjecting): The order has already been given . . . 150 were arrested yesterday afternoon.

GÖRING (continuing, to Heydrich): Otherwise, these things will be hidden. If somebody comes to a store and claims that he has bought them, they are to be confiscated at once. . . .

HEYDRICH: Looting was going on in the Reich in more than 800 [other] instances, contrary to what we supposed . . . we are trying to get the loot back.

GÖRING: And the jewels?

HEYDRICH: That is very difficult to say. They were partly thrown into the street and picked up there. Similar things happened with furriers. . . . There, the crowd rushed to pick up minks, skunks, and so forth. It will be most difficult to recover [the jewels]. Even children filled their pockets, just for fun.

65

The Third Reich's plundering, which persisted throughout the regime's reign, included objects of immense cultural value, but these, unlike the skunk skins and

Margraf wares of *Kristallnacht,* retained a traceability both during and after the war. The uniqueness of the objects ensured that, and this is strikingly confirmed in papers concerning Einsatzstab Rosenberg (Task Force Rosenberg), a project conceived for the purpose of seizing Jewish-owned art treasures in Nazi-occupied countries. Hitler himself took a personal interest in the project, and its chief, Reichsleiter Alfred Rosenberg, saw to it that *der Führer* was kept abreast of developments. Report after report makes clear that the identity and whereabouts of each stolen object were logged with utmost precision. In a report summarizing nearly four years of operations in France, one finds that 21,903 objects were confiscated and that each of them was "scientifically inventoried . . . and carefully packed by experts for transport to the Reich." Leaving no doubt as to the traceability of the booty, the report's author, an aide of Rosenberg's named Robert Scholz, writes, ". . . All seized articles of artistic value were photographed by the photography workshop of the task force and included in a film library. Thereby not only was the identity of each individual art work recorded but also there was created material of permanent value for study and publication. . . ." Entire libraries of Judaica and Hebraica, their combined volumes numbering in the hundreds of thousands, were stolen in the Netherlands, France, and Poland and shipped to Frankfurt-am-Main, where, documents tell us, the Nazis planned to establish a seminary (*Hohe Schule*) for study of "The Jewish Question."

In a decree issued January 29, 1940, to "all sections of Party and State," Hitler declared, "The seminary is intended to become the center for National Socialistic ideological and educational research. It will be established after the conclusion of the war. I order that the already initiated preparations be continued by Reichsleiter Rosenberg."

Predictably, Rosenberg's best shopping took place in France. His staff waxes rhapsodic in its praise of collections found in townhouses and castles belonging to the Rothschild family. A report states, "The paintings, period furniture of the seventeenth and eighteenth centuries, the Gobelins, the antiques and Renaissance jewelry of the Rothschilds are objects of so unique a character that their evaluation is impossible [to make], since no comparable values have so far appeared on the art market." As of July 15, 1944, an inventory shows, the Rothschilds and other wealthy families had lost thousands of oils, pastels, watercolors, and drawings, their creators among the most illustrious names known to Western civilization—Rembrandt, Rubens, Cranach, Vermeer, Goya, Watteau, Fragonard, Frans Hals. On April 16, 1943, four days before Hitler turned fifty-four, Rosenberg wrote him, "In my desire to give you, my Führer, some joy for your birthday, I take the liberty to present to you a portfolio containing photos of some of the most valuable paintings that my task force, in compliance with your order, has secured from ownerless Jewish art collections. This portfolio represents only a small percentage of these objects of art seized by my service command in France and now stored in a safe place in the Reich. . . . [It is] my hope that this all too brief distraction with the beautiful things of art, so near to your heart, will send a ray of beauty and joy into your revered life."

In Kaphammel's view, the restitution program has proceeded smoothly (a view challenged by Ernest M. Weismann, a veteran consultant to the Conference on Jewish Material Claims Against Germany). Initially, Kaphammel told me, his Ministry was so inundated with claims that the program required the services of thousands of employees, but the roster has now been drastically reduced. "Ninety-nine-point-five percent of the claims have been settled," Kaphammel said, consulting a paper on his desk. Compensation, he went on, is made in the form of either pensions or lump sums. The latter group encompasses loss of property, such as securities, bank accounts, jewelry, real estate. The group also includes emigration expenses and business losses suffered as the result of boycott, liquidation, and discriminatory taxes. A similar type of payment has been made for *Freiheitsschaden*—"loss of freedom." Examples of *Freiheitsschaden* run a wide gamut. Specifically, the Federal Republic has fined itself five marks (about two dollars, at today's rate of exchange) for each day that the Third Reich imprisoned someone in a concentration camp; two dollars has been levied for those forced to "hide," which is defined as living in "illegality under degrading conditions"; the same amount has gone to those who were deported to ghettos or made to wear Stars of David (whose equivalent, figuratively speaking, turned up in telephone directories, where Jewish subscribers were listed with either "Sara" or "Israel" added to their names).

Continuing, Kaphammel informed me that flat payments have been made to those whose education was interrupted. Thus, Kaphammel said, if a Jewish medical student was prevented from carrying on with his courses, he could gain up to ten thousand marks (about four thousand three hundred dollars) in *Wiedergutmachung* (and he could put in other claims as well, for such things as time spent in a camp). Flat payments have also been made to those—artists, writers, and scholars, for instance—whose education was completed but whose budding careers were wrecked for racial or political reasons. In contrast, claimants who were already well established in their professions have been remunerated for life by means of monthly pensions. All civil servants are in line for pensions, but in their case the imponderables that operate are such as to approach the fictional. No matter how long ago a civil servant may have fled Germany, no matter what other vocation he may have since embraced, the government assumes that he persevered in his old profession, as though the Third Reich had never existed. Another assumption, I learned, is that civil servants received "promotions" during their phantom careers, which, naturally, entitled them to larger pensions than they would have received otherwise. In one instance that I know of, a former Berlin judge, who has long been a resident of New York, received three "promotions," making his monthly pension equal to that of a presiding judge of a German court of appeals.

As might be expected, Kaphammel told me, adults who lost family breadwinners in camps have been given lifetime pensions. On the average, a widow's reimbursement comes to about seven hundred marks (a little over three hundred dollars) monthly; orphans received no money after their eighteenth birthday. Where whole families were exterminated, *Wiedergutmachung* was out of the question, there being no family members left to indemnify. Heirless properties, though, have not gone unclaimed. Through the operations of the Jewish Restitution Successor Organization, an executor-like agency formed in the United States by a dozen Jewish organizations, the properties, whose value came to about fifty million dollars, have been turned to a variety of philanthropic uses. One of them was the restoration of gutted synagogues and vandalized cemeteries, and another the tracing of more than ten thousand ceremonial objects, including a thousand Torah scrolls, made of parchment, that were charred or torn; scribes repaired the scrolls, which were then distributed to synagogues in Israel and Western Europe. Hundreds of plundered paintings were recovered, some of them finding homes at the Hebrew Union College in Cincinnati and at the Jewish Museum in New York. In Queens, New York, in 1963, *Wieder-*

70

gutmachung realized from heirless properties made possible the construction of a twelve-story residential building for elderly refugees from the Third Reich; a second building of nineteen stories was constructed in 1970. In Israel, agricultural settlements came into being, as did special schools for the study of Hebrew. In the Netherlands, in 1960, Queen Juliana attended the formal opening of a psychiatric hospital in the town of Amersfoort, its patients all Nazi victims.

Pensions, I learned, are mailed monthly to those who have suffered *Erwerbsverminderung*—"reduction in earning power"—as a result of imprisonment in concentration camps. A high percentage of former inmates have undergone *Erwerbsverminderung* because they were permanently disabled by beatings at the hands of S.S. guards; by medical experiments conducted by German physicians; by diseases that went untreated; by infections that led to amputations. Malnutrition, too, took its toll, I was informed, producing cretins and teen-age girls whose development as females has proved to be arrested. Liberated from camps, many survivors accepted freedom hampered by chronic psychological disorders (one of the most common being claustrophobia); often, I was told, the ring of a telephone late at night has caused former inmates to require medical assistance. On more than one occasion, it might be mentioned, litigants have submitted certified medical diagnoses with which the Ministry of Finance has disagreed; in situations of this kind, a third, and deciding, opinion has been sought.

Inevitably, the program has had its share of snarls, for at bottom it is probably a program that no one has wanted, neither benefactor nor beneficiary. The Federal Republic—the enforced benefactor—can hardly have relished being stuck with a bill run up by a defunct regime. And as for the program's beneficiaries, which of them would not gladly have forgone their compensation if they could have lived their lives without the interventions of Adolf Hitler? In any event, I learned from Kaphammel, thousands of appeals have been lodged by those who have felt they were being dealt with inadequately. Most often, litigation has involved *Erwerbsverminderung.* Further litigation, I learned, has resulted from the fact that, oddly, a class system has held sway in the world of *Wiedergutmachung,* as a result of which those who suffered identical injuries have not necessarily been awarded identical compensation. The disparity, it was explained, hinges on the economic background of the claimants. Thus, I was told, restitution for a former locksmith would be far less than that for a former brain surgeon, because they belong to different "categories," of which there are four: lower, medium, higher, high. Given this setup, it is not surprising that those in inferior categories strive, through litigation, to have themselves elevated to a higher category—all of which, Kaphammel observed, has kept government lawyers busy over the years. Nevertheless, he said, of the four and a half million claims filed by individuals, only fifteen thousand are still unresolved.

Halting his flow of information, Kaphammel indicated that he had probably given me as much of a backward look as was possible within the bounds of his work. He did go on to say that he had no way of telling how long the program of quantified atonement would continue. No doubt, he thought, that depended on attrition. "People die," Kaphammel said, reminding me that eventually the program will run out of heirs. Plans have been drawn that extend to the year 2000. If that seems overly foresighted, Kaphammel added, it might be well to bear in mind that his Ministry's clients are not subject to actuarial tables ordinarily employed by insurance companies. Medically speaking, he said, the clients are *widerstandsfähig*—"resistant to enfeeblement." "They survived the camps, they are among the physically hardy," he said.

7 *Der Nebel*

I left Bonn for Berlin, still the true capital of Germany—
both Germanys—and, in a sense, of the world, for what
other metropolis is there in which East and West meet
each day in wary contact, what other multinationally
occupied city is there whose seizure would almost certainly touch off an outbreak of war between superpowers?
A plane would have had me in Berlin in an hour, but I
caught a noon train, due to arrive in the early evening.
I was in no hurry; I wanted to take stock of what I had
been hearing for the past several days. Few passengers

were aboard—it was the middle of a holiday weekend—and I had no difficulty finding an empty compartment, which would afford me the solitude I was seeking. As the train began to move, I waved farewell to a short, gray-haired man who was seeing me off. He had driven me to the station from his home, a cottage in a village several miles outside Bonn. I had stayed there two days with him and his wife, a spirited, perceptive woman of sixty who taught philosophy at a university; her husband, who was disposed to silence, wrote about medieval manuscripts for bibliographic journals. I had been put on to the couple before leaving America, by a young friend whose mother, a Jew, had escaped the Nazis through the help of my hostess; throughout the war, my friend told me, she had assisted in the rescue of Jews. In the many hours we spent together, she herself never mentioned these activities, and, in fact, only once did the topic of the Third Reich come up. That was shortly before her husband drove me to the *Bahnhof*, when, standing in the doorway of her house, she wished me well in my pursuit of "a backward look." She spoke then of the profound disinclination on the part of Germans to recall the Hitler regime. Others had made the point to me, but none had expressed it so passionately. A pent-up scorn marked her words. Her hands tightened into fists, she said, "How *can* Germans talk about themselves? Are they to admit they were Nazis, for which they might be punished? Are they to confess their shame, their guilt? They know full well they were utter cowards for following a madman, for murdering—what other word is there?—millions of innocent, defenseless people. A fog—*ein Nebel*—clouds their heads. *Der Nebel* is always with them; they live in it. Once in a great while, I hear some man or woman talk about those filthy years, but when they do, God alone knows what their memories have to do with reality."

As the train gathered speed, *der Nebel* was very much on my mind. Perhaps there was such a fog as my hostess had described, but if there was, I decided, it wasn't peculiar to Germans. Aliens, too, were susceptible to it. Certainly I was, I knew, for it had been coming home to me strongly that the more I looked back on the Nazi era, the more murky and knotted were the thoughts it summoned. Naturally, they differed in kind from those that Germans might harbor. Unlike Lantin, for instance, the K.K.G. teacher who had pulled guard duty near Buchenwald, I did not have to lie awake with an ineradicable memory of having watched, unprotesting, running gangs of striped, shivering skeletons. I had never raised an arm in salute to Hitler or packed human beings into camp-bound cattle cars or sat reading beside a lampshade made of someone's tattooed skin or mined the mouths of asphyxiated inmates for gold fillings. No, it wasn't such acts from which my own fog emanated but, rather, from a single fact: an atrocity of unparalleled—of unprecedented—magnitude had been committed for years and years, deliberately and efficiently, and it was going unpunished. In a framework unrelated to the prosecution of war (as Frentz, the tall, bald, journalist, had noted), millions of people had been wiped out and thousands of others left to live on, reeling and envenomed, their days scarred beyond healing; and yet if one cast about for signs of retribution little more than a handful of show trials sprang to mind—and, of course, Kaphammel's pensions. In Aachen and Bonn, in Cologne and other cities, the sight of crowded German streets could give me a sense of witnessing complacent jailbreaks; surely, it seemed to me, many—perhaps a great many— of the jostling pedestrians and honking drivers, all going about their business, had had a hand in the unprecedented atrocity. But no dragnet, I knew, was in the offing—only questions fit for a fog. Staring out the train window, I again remembered Lantin telling about his January morning near Buchenwald. His stricken eyes had affected me, but that had been when we were alone, two men in conversation, in a small, disheveled study. There had been no backdrop of ongoing assembly-line slaughter, impersonal and bureaucratic. Necessarily, that element had been missing from our talk, but this didn't occur to me until after I left Lantin's house, for which I blamed the expression in his eyes. It was after I left his house, too, that an overwhelming question came hurtling at me: What if Hitler had won? Would anyone's eyes have been contrite? Would anyone have compared Hitler to the Devil?

My fog thickening, I wondered what effects, if any, the holocaust had left behind. Were they destined to save us, like a vaccination, from a recurrence of a similar dread disease? Or, once loosed, did they render us forever vulnerable? Had the holocaust breached the known limits of evil, uncovering fresh temptations, beckoning us to renew old acquaintance? Dilemmas were a dime a dozen; one could go on juggling them *ad infinitum*. Emunds, for instance, had said he liked to think that the subject he taught imparted "warnings" that, to paraphrase Santayana, we would do well to heed lest we repeat the errors of the past. Ah, but then there was Hegel's apothegm: "What experience and history teach is ... that people and governments have never learned anything from history." What could stuff like that possibly have to do with filling mattresses with the hair of inmates, with making soap of their fats? I rose and paced within the confines of my compartment. I felt an impatience with history and its worship of the past; it was a deliciously judgmental sport that added up to a pretentious cipher. Professor Haupts, I recalled, had revealed himself a shark at the game, arranging his knowledge so that Charlemagne and Hitler emerged as interchangeable characters, each bailing out the other. In effect, the professor had seemed to be saying, Our behavior doesn't matter, given the inexorable, lavalike flow of centuries. Amiably, adroitly, he had detached our lifespans from that flow, but to do that, it struck me, was to forget that it was only while we lived that we could affect time's course. In and of itself, looking back was an empty exercise. Our lives were events of immediacy. We had to act when it counted or lose our chance to touch time. If the exterminated had in fact left us a "warning," it was that, relentlessly, irreversibly, the present was at hand. The professor's son had appeared more conscious of that than his father. I remembered Michael's indignation at the notion that someone his age had any atonement to make for the nefarious works of the Third Reich. "I wasn't even born!" Michael had exclaimed, and he was right—most assuredly, each generation fended for itself. In Jerusalem, in 1967, I heard a boy of Michael's age upbraid his Polish parents, both survivors of Treblinka. They had been going on at length about the camp when, impatiently, the boy had snapped, "Enough, enough! I forgive you!"

8 *The Old Capital*

Berlin was a dizzying kaleidoscope. Nothing seemed to happen in an ordinary way. My first morning, rising in my hotel room, I tried to reach Heinz Galinski, head of the local *Jüdische Gemeinde,* or Jewish Community, a formal organization representing most of the city's Jews. Galinski, I believed, would be in a position to tell me how Jews were faring in the old capital. His office was closed for the holiday weekend, so I rang a common acquaintance for Galinski's home number. The acquaintance, his voice low, told me, "I can't give it to you. The

Arabs are after Galinski." He suggested that we meet for a drink later on at the Kempinski, a well-known hotel, and I agreed. Before meeting him, I went on a bus tour, and, among other places, the coach stopped at the once-notorious Plötzensee prison, where the Nazis had tormented political opponents. Torture devices were on display, and in front of them a group of teen-agers stood laughing uproariously; one of their number had made a lewd joke about a particular device. Outraged, our guide, a man in his middle years, cut short our visit, resolutely leading us back to the bus. I had lunch in a crowded cafeteria on the Kurfürstendamm. A dowdy, beaming woman descended on an unoccupied place opposite me. She could hardly wait to tell me her age. "I'm sixty," she announced, sitting down. She was from East Berlin, whose travel restrictions had kept her from visiting West Germany for more than twenty years. She had turned sixty a month ago, and after attaining this age, it appeared, East Germans were free to travel anywhere. In fact, the government would just as soon they kept right on traveling—they were considered unproductive workers, and their welfare costs were a drain on the exchequer. "It's such a pleasure to be on this side of the wall," the woman said. In an hour, she would be leaving for Hannover to visit a brother, a lapsed Communist. She said, "Two weeks with him, then I'll go back to East Berlin. It's my home. I'm used to it. I'm sixty. Where else can someone like me go?"

At the Kempinski, my acquaintance and I had drinks

in the lobby while a tea dance was in progress in a room just out of our line of vision. A small band was playing ancient tunes—"You Are My Sunshine," "Melancholy Baby," "Honeysuckle Rose." My companion, a Jew, was the same age as ex-*Flakhelfer* I had met. He was an executive in the Berlin branch of an American firm; he lived, with his wife and children, in a comfortable apartment in a good district. He was an American citizen now, but he had been born in Germany, from which he and his parents had fled to the States in 1939. Our meeting seemed to put him on edge, for at its outset he made me pledge twice to refrain from quoting him by name. I thought that perhaps he was about to say something startling, but when he spoke it was to sing the praises of the Federal Republic of Germany. It had been kind to Jews, he said, and they should be thankful. He hoped that nothing would occur that might bring on pogroms— events that he had endured as a boy and would never forget. He cited the benefactions of *Wiedergutmachung,* adding that the government in Bonn was indiscriminate in its generosity, frequently extending it to people who in his opinion weren't entitled to it. Continuing his paean, he said that many German Jews who had found a haven in America had chosen to come back to their native land; if I wished, he said, I could find some of them in one of two homes for the aged that Galinski's organization maintained. He said, "Who would have dreamed that the climate for Jews would be good again in Germany? It's better than it was before Hitler." We rose and walked in

82

the direction of the tea dance. A dozen couples were on the floor, and half as many were relaxing at tables laden with food. Everyone present appeared to be about my companion's age. The women were nearly all buxom, bejeweled, overdressed, with conspicuous eye makeup. The dancing was sedately athletic, the men leading their partners with determination, wearing fixed smiles, eager to exchange greetings with anyone. My ex-refugee friend frowned at the assemblage. Speaking more to himself than to me, he said, "Tea dancing at the Kempinski. This goes on every day. They're all Jews." He seemed to remember my presence and turned to face me. An instant later, his features gave way to a weak grin, and, barely saying goodbye, he walked away.

The following day—the long weekend's last—I had a lunch date, but before keeping it I made a brief visit to a home for the aged that was a part of Galinski's organization. It appeared to be a clean, well-run institution, and it housed a hundred and twenty elderly people, a number of them married couples. I talked with a few of those who had returned from the States, all of them several years back. Unlike the man I had been with at the Kempinski, they did not think of the Federal Republic as a fount of beneficence but, rather, as a mechanism for providing funds to see them through their senescence. Certainly there was no disposition to regard the government's payments in any redemptive light as far as the vicissitudes that had befallen them under Hitler were concerned. One frail man in his eighties who had lived in Queens for many years told me with pride of fellow-refugees who had refused to apply for *Wiedergutmachung;* some of these friends had vowed never to set foot in Germany again. He wished he could emulate them, but, alas, he said, *"Alle von uns sind nicht Helden"* ("All of us are not heroes"). Another octogenarian ascribed his return to economics, no more, no less. Had he stayed on in America, he explained, he would have become a financial burden to his children; medical aid and living in an old-age home were more costly propositions in America than in the Federal Republic. Another reason for returning, it appeared, was a nostalgia for Berlin. Walled city though it was now, one could be reunited there with friends who had come back from scattered points around the globe and from other parts of Germany. A former bookkeeper and his wife told me they had missed friends of theirs who were Christian. They owed their lives to one of them—a man who had fashioned a hiding place for the pair under the debris of a synagogue destroyed in an air raid. The Christian had brought them food for months, then helped spirit them out of Germany. The former bookkeeper's wife, a slight, blue-eyed woman, said that it hadn't been easy to leave America, where she and her husband had children and grandchildren, but that the pull of the German language and culture, of old streets and familiar foods, had proved powerful; she assured me that the same pull had operated for the other people in the home who had returned from distant places. She said, "The memories of childhood are stronger than those of Hitler. Besides, time has passed, new generations have been born. We must go forward, even we whose future is short."

My lunch date had been made from the other side of the Atlantic. A neighbor of mine, a refugee whose grandparents had owned a prosperous department store in Westphalia, had written to married friends—Clara and Karl Hartmann, to use pseudonyms—of my impending visit. The three had met as fellow-passengers aboard a cruise ship plying the Greek islands; they had hit it off famously and were now planning a joint visit to Australia. The Hartmanns brought their daughter Lili, a shy, blond high-school student of seventeen, along to lunch. We ate in a Yugoslav restaurant, and it didn't take me long to see how my neighbor might have been attracted to the Hartmanns. Like him, the pair were extremely well read and on easy terms with the arts. Mrs. Hartmann, a handsome woman in her early fifties, was an actress with a long career; as she mentioned at one point, however, she had never been able to land a sizable part. Her husband was a lawyer, a mammoth, fair-haired man with a genial air. Our talk was forced but pleasant, most of it concerned with entertainments that I might take in before leaving Berlin. Over dessert, though, the conversation slipped into a different key when, politely, Hartmann asked what had brought me to Germany. I spoke sketchily of *Mit 15 an die Kanonen*, and after a moment's pause Mrs. Hartmann said, "Karl had a terrible time in the war. He was mistaken for a Jew." His surname, it seemed, was sometimes associated with Jews, and, for whatever reason, a Nazi official had suspected her husband, then a government employee, of passing as an Aryan. Hartmann's "case," I was told, had taken on an extra dimension when it was established that a late uncle of his had been a well-known Communist. For four months, it had been touch and go whether Hartmann would be trundled off to a concentration camp. Eventually, though, all had worked out well. Hartmann had been able to disprove the charge of being Jewish, and had spent the war as a legal officer in a Bavarian backwater that was of no interest to Allied bomber crews. Hartmann laughed reminiscently, for which his wife addressed him reproachfully. "You had a dreadful experience. Think what might have happened," she told him. Hartmann laughed again, saying, "Ridiculous, wasn't it, the idea that I could be a Jew? They're so emotional."

"But they're also good businessmen," Lili put in shyly, her voice scarcely above a whisper. "In my class in school, Jewish girls have clothes that cost much more than ours. Their clothes are prettier than ours. Even so, we try to be friendly to Jewish girls, but they are not friendly back. They stay to themselves, maybe because of their clothes."

"Lili is right," Mrs. Hartmann said "They have made fortunes in films and television. They are the ones who decide which actors get the big parts."

Outside the restaurant, before the Hartmanns and I went our separate ways, Mrs. Hartmann told me that she and her husband were eagerly awaiting their trip to

Australia with our common friend. Extending her hand, she said, "Please tell him that. Please give him our warmest greetings—*sehr schön grüssen lassen*."

I spent the remainder of the day in the company of a friend, Paul Moor, a writer from Texas who has lived in Germany for twenty-six years. It was a leafy spring afternoon, and we walked awhile in the Tiergarten—Berlin's Central Park. Young Maoists were out in force distributing handbills that called on everyone to fight for earthly paradise. We heard march music, and, moving toward its source, found a brass band holding forth on the stage of a bandshell. Out front were hundreds of families at picnic tables, many in the audience waving steins of beer in time to the music; children scampered everywhere. We wandered through zoo houses, on the walls of which, opposite exotic birds and nervous leopards, were photographs exhibiting the damage that Allied bombers had inflicted on the menagerie. Later, Paul drove me around the city in his car, showing me much of *die Mauer*—"the wall," twenty-eight miles long, that the German Democratic Republic, the Communist government of East Germany, had built in 1961 to halt the westward exodus of its citizens. In Wedding, a working-class neighborhood, we left Paul's car and climbed the steps of a wooden observation post that the Federal Republic had erected. Confronting us was a section of the wall, gray concrete ten feet high, at whose base were a half-dozen or so black wreaths commemorating those who had been shot by Communist police while they were trying to reach West Berlin. Four feet on the other side of the wall, immediately in front of us, stood another, and lower, wall, and beyond that, as we could see from our high vantage point, lay a broad strip of plowed ground, its surface broken here and there by tank traps; paralleling the plowed ground was a narrow strip of asphalt for the use of motorized patrols.` Still more obstacles awaited would-be refugees, for after the asphalt strip came a fence of electrified barbed wire. Attack dogs prowled on the other side of the fence. A final wall—the third—completed the formidable no man's land. In all, it was only twenty yards wide, but, staring beyond it into the streets of East Berlin, I had a sense of glimpsing another world—one in which the thought of flight, actual or suppressed or rejected, was a part of daily life. I was thinking this as we were about to descend from our wooden perch when Paul informed me that he had arranged for me to be taken on a quick tour of East Berlin late the following morning. My guide, he said, would be an Englishman he had known a long time— John Peet, who had covered Germany for Reuters, the British news agency; to the plaudits of the Communist press, Peet had gone over to East Berlin more than twenty-five years ago, well before *die Mauer* was constructed.

Early the next day, the holiday break finally at an end, I rang Galinski for an appointment. A secretary answered, and, after I had waited some minutes, she told me, "Mr. Galinski says he can see you in two weeks." Impatient to see him, I left at once for his headquarters at the Jüdische Gemeindehaus, which turned out to be a postwar building, two stories high, that had a beige façade; it stood on the site of a synagogue that Nazis had burned to the ground on *Kristallnacht*—the two-day rampage in November, 1938, when throughout Germany mobs had smashed and set fire to Jewish-owned property. In the lobby of the Gemeindehaus, I informed an armed guard I wished to see Galinski. As I was saying this, a stocky man in his sixties who was passing by stopped short and looked me up and down. With a half sigh, he said resignedly, "Come, come. I'll be just as busy two weeks from now as I am today." It was Galinski. He led me rapidly to his office, where, indulging in no amenities whatever, he told me to fire away. I asked whether the persecution of Jews under the Third Reich had left many Germans with a sense of guilt. Galinski shook his head. "Only a low percentage, and mostly, I believe, among older people," he replied.

Did he think anti-Semitism persisted in Germany?

Weighing his words, he said, "Yes, in a more or less clandestine way, and, again, mostly among older people. Others disagree with me, but I myself do not believe that in our times there will be a return of what once was. Our official attitude is that we are German Jews who are ready to take a constructive part in German life." Of course, Galinski pointed out, targets for anti-Semitism were not plentiful; not many Jews were around, either in West Germany or in East Germany. In pre-Nazi days, he said, Berlin's Jewish community totaled a hundred and seventy thousand; today the figure was six thousand, including the Jews in East Berlin. In all of West Germany, there were only twenty-nine thousand Jews, predominantly elderly, and in all of East Germany there were only two thousand. Nor, Galinski added, did any marked influx of Jews appear to be in the cards. He did not care to guess whether there lay ahead the posthumous realization of one of Hitler's most cherished dreams: a Jewless Germany.

I inquired what future Galinski saw for his community, and he replied brusquely, "I am not a prophet. My future is now—this very minute. That is what I work for." There was much to be done, he went on, naming, among other matters, the keeping up of the old-age homes, a cemetery, a kosher restaurant, and a school where children could study their religion. He shifted restlessly, his demeanor indicating that he wanted to get on with ministering to the needs of his dwindling community—he had been at it practically since the end of the war. And before that, as I knew, he had spent years as an inmate of three camps. Apparently, the experience had made of him a professional survivor, his mission now to help others survive. Galinski and I pushed back our chairs simultaneously and, moving toward the door, hurriedly took leave of each other.

I crossed into East Berlin at Checkpoint Charlie, a process that required more than a half hour, owing to bureaucratic torpor. Minutes afterward, I was in the thick of the Communist capital's traffic, the passenger of John Peet, who was driving a Czech car, a balky red Škoda. Peet, friendly and intelligent, had an engaging manner. He was tall and bearded, his eyes blue and alert. He was disposed to speak in a light, brittle way, despite an underlying seriousness. He looked younger than his age, which I took to be in the early sixties; Paul Moor had mentioned that Peet fought in the Spanish Civil War, more than forty years ago, as a member of the International Brigade, formed in 1936. He was married to a Bulgarian and had two children. At no point, as I had suspected might be the case, did he push any propaganda messages, which is not to say that every now and then he didn't make his political sympathies known. Thus, when I called the wall an abomination he retorted airily, "Who needs to go to West Berlin for a cowboy film?"

Peet made an attentive guide. As we drove past a squat, massive building, he said, "That's where Göring had his Air Ministry. I don't know how it wasn't destroyed—so much of the area right around it was." Not far from there, Peet indicated the site of the old Adlon, once Berlin's most fashionable hotel, going back to the days of the Kaisers; only its servants' wing had escaped obliteration, and this was now functioning as a small hotel. Driving along the Wilhelmstrasse, we were on the avenue where Hitler's chancellery had stood, and when we were on Unter den Linden we were seeing a tree-lined boulevard where generations of Germans had promenaded. The broad-leaved lindens conveyed an air of tranquillity, which was welcome, for East Berlin, the day I was there, was a noisy place. Much building was going on, including the construction of several foreign embassies. The traffic was heavy with large vehicles, an inordinate number of them tourist coaches. Peet pulled over and parked at the Alexanderplatz, the heart of East Berlin and formerly, before the wall, of all Berlin. It was a huge plaza, rimmed by shops and dominated by a television tower, a slender turret three hundred and sixty-five meters high, taller than the Eiffel Tower, with a slowly revolving restaurant at its pinnacle. Peet wanted me to see the sweeping view it afforded, but we were out of luck. A queue of hundreds was ahead of us, and it was being lengthened by tourists pouring out of buses parked in the vicinity. Taking note of the buses, Peet said that organized tours were very much a part of the local scene. Many of them consisted of nationals from sister Socialist states, come to pay their respects to the German Democratic Republic, perhaps the Soviet Union's most willing satellite. Among the visitors were some Westerners. It was not East Berlin alone that attracted the international travelers. A number of the buses, I learned from Peet, were bound for the Sachsenhausen and Ravensbrück concentration camps, an hour or so from East Berlin.

Peet's wife had been an inmate of Ravensbrück. Survivors and the relatives and friends of nonsurvivors were among the pilgrims seeking, vainly, to reclaim the fugitive past; I probably had done the same in going to Henri-Chapelle.

Neither Peet nor his wife was Jewish, but mention of the camps seemed to put him in mind of Jews. Standing in the Alexanderplatz, he said that there were only about four hundred Jews in East Berlin and that they were dying off. He told me that Galinski's opposite number there was a neurologist who carried out the job on a part-time basis; on high holidays, a cantor came over from West Berlin to sing at services, and a certified slaughterer flew up from Budapest once a week to kill poultry in accordance with Jewish dietary laws.

We returned to the Škoda, and Peet drove intently for a few minutes to the Grosse Hamburgerstrasse, a side street, where we got out. Berlin's oldest Jewish home for the aged and oldest cemetery had been there, the latter having fallen into disuse in 1827. Little was left of either place. Tucked away from the city, the site formed a grassy refuge, much of it having been turned into a small park since the end of the war. Peet seemed drawn to the enclave. He had been there many times before, to judge by his easy knowledge of the place. As we walked about, he spoke of its few relics with an archeologist's regard. He showed me the headstone of Moses Mendelssohn, bearing the Jewish philosopher's dates: 1729–1786. His was the sole headstone to be found, and, at that, it appeared, it was but a reconstruction of the original, the Nazis having all but done away with the cemetery in 1943. In the final, frenzied days of Berlin's capture, Peet informed me, it had served again, briefly, as a burial ground; fallen defenders of the capital had been interred in the old Jewish graveyard, among them twenty or thirty members of the Gestapo. Several years ago, in 1972, their bodies had been exhumed and placed elsewhere.

As we passed a park bench occupied by a man and his young son, Peet pointed ahead to a memorial stone of red granite that was flanked by urns and pillars. An inscription on the stone recorded that the Gestapo had employed the Jewish home for the aged as a collecting headquarters for the deportation of German Jews. "From here," the inscription said, "the fascists abducted more than 50,000 Jewish human beings, from nursing infants to old men and women, to the concentration camps at Auschwitz and Theresienstadt, where they were bestially murdered. Never forget that!" When I had finished reading the literally lapidary message, Peet observed that the Jews to which it referred had all been of German origin and that their incarceration had followed that of the Jews of Poland, Hungary, and other countries under Nazi rule. Wryly, he suggested that perhaps this saving of homegrown victims for the last had come down to a piece of German nationalism. He looked up at the rear windows of a series of apartment houses, the façades of which were shedding plaster. There were scores of windows, and they afforded an unimpeded view of the area from which the home and the graveyard had vanished. What scenes, Peet exclaimed, the wartime tenants of those flats had stared down upon from their windows! Day in and day out, he said, the tenants—hundreds of them—had been able to witness Gestapo men herding hordes of Jews into waiting lorries. Perhaps, Peet granted, these neighbors may have been ignorant of the precise fate that lay in store for the captives, but nothing, he insisted, could ever persuade him that the onlookers hadn't known they were watching the deportation of "more than 50,000 Jewish human beings, from nursing infants to old men and women." Nor were the mass departures merely a matter of neighborhood gossip. The Grosse Hamburgerstrasse was practically at the center of Berlin. "The Adlon was ten minutes from here, the Alexanderplatz five," Peet said. His tone had lost its brittle edge. He had been speaking urgently, almost rhythmically, and the more he spoke, the more his words reminded me that the Nazis had got away with their evil. As had already occurred to me, millions of them were at large, indebted for their amnesty to the simple passage of time—time that had steadily, remorselessly erased the traces of their myriad malefactions. The K.K.G. boys, with their changing voices, weren't even aware that any evidence had to be destroyed; to them the Third Reich was homework, like geography and Latin. To those of *Flakhelfer* vintage, though, and to their elders—to Haupts, Lantin, Pastor Fuchs, and the other deponents of *Mit 15 an die Kanonen*—a backward look was something else again. It involved memories that had to be screened and suited to the needs of the present, for the present was as all-consuming now as it had been in the time of Hitler; it was only right now, as we tried to keep going, that we had a chance to acquire merit in our own eyes—no other

95

minute counted. Could ordinary circumstances test our mettle? Or did it take rampant inhumanity? Political enemies though we were, I felt a momentary kinship with Peet. Standing together where we were, the two of us shared the risk of giving in to an old and pernicious illusion; namely, that contemplating the sins of the past was an absolving force for the living. One had to earn the right to mourn. Otherwise, all was a matter of letting bygones be bygones, of practicing an acceptance that could only lead to repetition.

In the distance, from the direction of the Alexanderplatz, a vehicle backfired. It was a bus, I decided. What port of history was it bound for—Sachsenhausen or Warsaw or Paris? I imagined that the traffic on Unter den Linden was made up of nothing but buses, packed and going every which way; in another moment, a great cacophony of their horns would begin to rend the air.

Response

When most of "A Backward Look" appeared in *The New Yorker*, the response to it took me by surprise. Somewhat like Emunds' paperback, the account seemed to touch a nerve, in the history teacher's phrase, and perhaps now that the story is in book form it may be in order to tell of that response. "A Backward Look" was barely out when my phone began to ring and mail to arrive; people I scarcely knew stopped me to discuss Nazis; my typewriter repairman of many years, hitherto silent and remote, informed me that he was a survivor of the concentration camp at Bergen-Belsen. It was the letters, though, that persuaded me that conceivably a nerve had been touched. Dozens of them came in, impressing me not only by their number but by their intensity and thoughtfulness. As might be expected, much of this correspondence was from people who had fled the Third Reich, but Americans also wrote, their addresses concentrated in no particular section of the country. From the Midwest, for example, I heard from a former Army officer, who upon the German surrender had served as "the town major," or military mayor, in Koblenz, the Rhine city where Emunds' students had investigated governmental archives in connection with putting together *Mit 15 an die Kanonen*. Reminiscently, the ex-town major, now an Ohio businessman, wanted me to know that he had not had a religious upbringing but that he had witnessed the liberation of Auschwitz "and I have had religion ever since." A novelist living in the East— Robert Crichton, author of *The Secret of Santa Vittoria*— let me know that, as an infantryman, he had helped capture Aachen and, concomitantly, a number of *Flak-helfer*, many of whom had fought bravely. Crichton wrote, "Once they gave up, I was embarrassed by their age and the size of some of them." And from Memphis, in the South, the mother of a four-year-old wrote that she and her husband had chosen a Jewish friend—a native American—as the godfather of their child. Recently, she wrote, the friend had said something odd: "He told me I spent an inordinate amount of time reading about Nazis."

The letters took in a broad range. Some were recollections, pure and simple, their contents direct and affecting. Others had a brooding, inward tone, and still others adopted an analytical air, striving, as it were, to lend shape to all that had happened under Hitler. But perhaps the letters should be permitted to speak for themselves. Reading and rereading them, as I have done, I find that they give me a sense of not having finished writing "A Backward Look"; they create an illusion for me that others have assumed that task. One letter, in fact, is almost literally a continuation of "A Backward Look," taking up exactly where the published story left off—in East Berlin, in the Grosse Hamburgerstrasse, in the small park where John Peet had recalled for me the war's shocks to the Jewish cemetery and to the home for the aged. The correspondent in this instance, Ingrid Loebel, a native Berliner, had been a schoolgirl in that very spot. Now the wife of a violinist with the Cleveland Orchestra, she wrote that since the war she had been to Germany once, in 1975, touring it with the orchestra, but that her "courage" had failed her when it came to seeing Berlin again. Her letter, I think, gives some idea of how that could have come about:

"I grew up in what is now East Berlin and for four years, from 1934, at the age of ten, to late 1938, went to school there at the *Mittelschule der Jüdischen Gemeinde* [the Middle School of the Jewish Community]. The building stood directly adjacent to the girls' classrooms in front of the school building, with a boys' wing across the courtyard, which was off limits to girls. We had to parade around the rear schoolyard during recess. The cemetery was separated from the rear schoolyard by a low fence and a small gate.

"As Nazi laws became more restrictive and Jewish youngsters were forbidden to attend German schools, public or private, the enrollment in the *Mittelschule* soared beyond the capacity of the building, which was 100 years old, as was the school itself. In addition, students were sent from small towns to attend school in Berlin; parents in the provinces believed that, in contrast to what was happening in their towns, it was unlikely that anti-Semitic outbursts would occur in the capital.

"When the schoolyard became too small for the enlarged group, the administration changed the rules, allowing older boys and girls to take their daily walk around the cemetery. We felt privileged and very grown up. The cemetery was our park, and since now we had only a gymnasium that had become too small, the cemetery was pressed into use as our athletic field. We did the 100-meter dash next to the wall which surrounded the old graveyard. It seemed sacrilegious and out of place to run along the old grave markers, the large headstone of Moses Mendelssohn looming above the rest. But we did, in our brief gym suits with our teacher standing at the end of the path, stopwatch in hand, wearing bloomers down to her knees, like an old-fashioned bathing costume. We were crazy about Jesse Owens, the American sprinter, and thought we could come close to his record at the 1936 Olympics. I thought it was cruel to have the home for the aged next to the cemetery, but we must have provided some diversion for the old people, many of whom watched us at our games.

"I shall never forget my last day at the *Mittelschule*. The date was November 10th, 1938. *Kristallnacht* had turned into *Kristalltag*. I walked to school very frightened. On the way, I saw a firetruck turning away from a burning synagogue. Only a handful of girls showed up. Our first class was shorthand. The teacher admonished us to pay attention, saying again and again, 'We are all nervous today. Please try.' But shorthand seemed ridiculous. I had great trouble concentrating on little symbols I might never need. At the end of the lesson, we were told it would be better if we went home. The administration worried about our safety. I remember standing in the high vaulted hallway, each of us awaiting her turn to leave the building with another girl. We did so five minutes apart, so as not to attract attention. On the way home, we saw many Jewish shops being looted. From that evening on until the day we left Berlin two weeks later, I saw open trucks filled to capacity with men sitting on benches, guarded by Nazis in uniform, being driven in the direction of the railroad station. The men seemed very quiet. One of them waved to me. Who was it? I think of him to this day. And I wonder, too, about my teachers. What happened to them? They wanted to be the last to leave.

"On November 28th, 1938, my mother, sister, and I were smuggled across the border into Belgium."

From other refugees born in Germany, I received a number of letters written in a quite different tone from that of the violinist's wife. Curiously, or so it seemed to me, those letters shared a sense of thwarted nationalism—and I do not mean *Heimweh*, or homesickness, for the old country. Recurrently, in this mail, reference was made to past patriotic service, to medals earned in the First World War, to legs lost by distant forebears in Bismarck's day. The letters are naked in their melancholy, their authors expressing not outrage at having been persecuted but, rather, disappointment at having been rejected by the Fatherland, like children cast out of a family to which they dearly wanted to belong. How *could* their own, their cherished land have sent them packing for such flimsy, transient matters as race and politics! One letter in particular stands out for me, its lines hurt and confused, its readiness to find fault with America—the Fatherland's conqueror—all too apparent. The sender's birthplace was Aachen, the same as Emunds' and the K.K.G. boys' who had been *Flakhelfer.* The letter came from California; here it is, practically in its entirety:

"I left Aachen in 1938 at the age of seventeen under far from happy circumstances, yet I keep having ambivalent feelings. I take a rather simple-minded pleasure in the fact that the spelling of the city's name gives it first place in most encyclopediae. But more importantly, my family had a business there for over a hundred years: Aachen *was* home—deep down it still is.

"'A Backward Look' treated subjects I have thought about a lot, especially guilt. My earlier feelings toward Germans—blanket hatred—have undergone a radical change, largely through a rather thorough grounding in *American* history: Show me the Americans who spoke out against the lynchings of blacks (or other minorities); show me the Americans who spoke out against putting Indians into reservations, which, in many cases, were deserts; show me the Americans who spoke out against putting Japanese into so-called relocation centers in World War II. I know there were some—damn few!—just as there were some Germans who spoke out or did 'little things.' (Our chauffeur in Aachen was one; he helped smuggle out some of our belongings.)

"Just the same, I have never gone back. I went through Aachen a few years ago on a train from Copenhagen to Paris. I stood at the window looking at the skyline with indescribable emotions. Last year, in Paris, I saw a tour bus from Aachen and later burst into tears, mortifying my American wife. Damn! That's not all: Until we were told we were not wanted, we were good Germans. My father received an Iron Cross in World War I. One of his brothers and one of my mother's brothers died in that war, and I was named after them. How does one shake that off? I think I haven't yet."

In an offstage way, two mathematicians, both women, have figured in my experience with "A Backward Look"— and an experience it has been. One of the mathematicians had been a college classmate of my hostess in Bonn—the Christian who had spirited Jews out of Germany during "those filthy years," as she termed Hitler's reign. As may be recalled, it was this hostess who asserted to me that

103

Germans of that period now lived their lives in *einem Nebel*—a fog—when it came to thinking, or not thinking, of the Third Reich. She had just set forth this view when, digressing momentarily, she remembered her mathematician classmate, whom she described as being a generally well-balanced, civilized person who took no stock in anti-Semitism or other such Nazi articles of faith. But even Germans of this solid sort, it appeared, could be caught up in the heady victories that marked the early phase of Hitler's accession to power, for whenever *der Führer*'s name was mentioned, I was told, the mathematician's face would light up, her manner one of glowing admiration. One day my hostess finally called her on this, and, soberly and sounding logical, the mathematician responded, "Hitler cannot be explained. He is a miracle. He is like a given in an equation that cannot be solved, he is like the will of destiny itself in whose path no one can stand."

The second mathematician was among the letter writers. America has been her home since 1934, when, as a young girl, she quit Germany; she is now an associate professor at the University of California. My hostess's metaphor of *ein Nebel* had set her thinking, and the object of the mathematician's letter was to elaborate on it, to give it anatomy. It was her belief, she wrote, that the wartime followers of Hitler had not got off unscathed, regardless of how thriving an appearance they might now present. Her letter reads:.

"The central fact of 'A Backward Look,' I believe, is

'der Nebel'. If you will use the technical term 'repression,' it will help a lot. Repression is the mechanism which allows people to live with *unbearable* experiences—you blot them out before they come to awareness. All those people you interviewed owe the fog in which they now live to the 'forgetting' they did in the Hitler era, the 'forgetting' that made it possible for them then to 'go along' or 'not know.' Over the years, I have spent time talking with German visitors, usually mathematicians and scientists, who come over regularly. These visitors not only stayed on in Germany during the war but worked in universities and for their war effort. Now and then, over drinks, they admit to feelings of guilt but they ask, 'What could we *do?*' On those occasions when we have continued our conversations beyond this point, we have got into how carelessly the Americans bombed, how barbarous the Russians were ('animals') and finally— often, though still a little veiled—'Versailles' and 'It was America's fault.' But basically, it is all a matter of repression, or fog. The price of repression is *very* high. The punishment is automatic: repression demands a shutting off of large parts of the mind, the giving up of much intelligence and creativity—it is a terrible self-crippling. The people you talked with all suffer in one way or another from what they did or omitted to do."

The mail that came in included yet another letter taken up with "forgetting"; it came from a native American living in a Western state. Unlike the mathematician, the writer was not concerned with psychological matters, with explaining the behavior of Germans who had chosen to "go along" or "not know." On the contrary, she was preoccupied with paying tribute to—with not forgetting—those Germans who had acquitted themselves decently and bravely; she assumed they numbered in the hundreds. Nor, she emphasized, was it outstanding heroes she had in mind but, rather, ordinary, unsung people who had acted on their own at moments when it mattered to someone else. The Westerner wrote, "I have never heard of a monument to the hundreds of men and women whose help, maybe just a small help, made it possible for someone to live who would otherwise have been killed. I don't imagine these men and women can forget so easily. I imagine they sometimes wake up in the night terribly frightened, forgetting that it's not 1943 any more. Their names should be inscribed for the youth to emulate their courage. I think of the monument as something like a fountain of pure water in a dirty city. I think I would write on the monument the line, 'You, the honor of a people!' Perhaps because of the holocaust, a few deaths more or less pass without notice, but whenever a person dies because of *choosing* to risk death doing a noble act, that death is a precious talisman for the whole human race. What good does it do to claim a conscience if one doesn't use it when it makes the difference between someone's living or dying? Is a conscience just for self-flagellation?"

In general, the letters I received from native Americans, like that of the Westerner just quoted, lacked the scarred involvement with Germany that characterized those written by refugees. By definition, the Americans' communications were those of *Ausländer*—outlanders, literally, as Germans call foreigners—and, almost as though to prove it, the communications were often the product of tourism. Sometimes the tourism didn't even have anything to do with Germany itself, as in the case of an Arizonian who, on reading "A Backward Look," wrote me about an organized bus tour she had made of Galilee. All the passengers had been American Jews, except for a young German couple who had come to Israel for their honeymoon. In the course of the trip, which had taken three days, the Arizonian wrote, she had watched a feeling of affection toward the newlyweds spring up on the part of the Jews. The Arizonian wrote, "No one in the group talked of anything in regard to Nazi Germany. It was obvious the two youngsters had been born long after the war. The passengers took delight in teasing the honeymooners. They were always late in the morning for the tour. They would hurry aboard, still sleepy, their hands holding their breakfasts of fruit and rolls that they hadn't yet eaten."

The travel of young Germans figured again, this time extensively and bizarrely, in communications sent me by a Viennese, Stella K. Hershan, who had found sanctuary in America as a young woman, in 1938. She wrote me twice, initially to say that in reading "A Backward Look" she had been especially interested in the reactions to the Hitler regime that I had encountered among young people in Germany. Her interest, she explained, lay in the fact that "I myself am involved in a study of the emotions of young Germans now working temporarily in New York at the United Nations, government offices of the Federal Republic, and German firms such as the Mercedes-Benz Company." It was not until I heard from Mrs. Hershan again, a month later, that I had any idea what her study had been turning up. I learned it from a half dozen "case histories" she sent me; many times that number were in her possession. Overwhelmingly, they bore out a single point. Mrs. Hershan wrote, "Unlike the young people you met in their homeland, young Germans become aware of the horror of the Hitler period only once they are in a foreign country and especially in New York. Without any guilt of their own, these children of the Nazi generation, I have observed, now consider themselves in a situation that may cast a shadow over their entire life."

I looked through the case histories; here are excerpts from four of them:

(1) "Christina T., a pretty woman of about thirty; she is from Frankfurt and presently employed as a public relations director for a German concern in New York.

"Christina has stated, 'I felt very much alone on my first day in New York. It was a Saturday and my job did not begin until Monday. I did not know anyone here. Walking through the streets of this enormous city was exciting but also intimidating. I went into a coffee shop called Heidi's. The name sounded friendly and homelike. As soon as I sat down at the counter I heard two ladies next to me speaking German. I was so happy to hear my own language spoken in this big foreign city that I turned to them and introduced myself in German. But they looked at me with great hostility and said that they did not want to have anything to do with Germans. I had no idea what they were talking about. But then I saw one woman's arm resting in her lap. There was a purple number tattooed on it. She noticed my stare. 'Your people did that,' she said. 'They murdered thousands. I happen to be a survivor who was not gassed.' I found a bathroom, where I was sick. Since living in New York, I try to read anything I can about what took place. I have found a psychiatrist. She is a German Jew and she keeps telling me that I do not have to feel guilty, that I was born after the Nazis fell from power. But what about my parents? What part did they play? They have never told me. They have acted as though Hitler never lived. How will I face them when I go back to Germany?'

(2) "Ingrid G., thirty-two, from Munich; she is in the United States as a marketing researcher with a textile firm.

"Ingrid has stated, 'I first heard about things that the Nazis had done when I was eight. There was this little girl who came to school day after day weeping. I finally asked her what was the matter, and she said that her father had just been imprisoned as a war criminal. He had been accused of killing hundreds of inmates in a camp. I raced home and blurted to my father, '*Her* father did this! Did you do it, too?' There was a terrible scene. My mother said to me, 'How dare you speak with such disrespect! I forbid you ever to bring up the subject again.' To this day, I have not had the courage to confront them a second time.'

(3) "Rosemarie L., twenty-eight, born in a small town in Saxony, now employed as a secretary in New York.

"Rosemarie's father, an engineer, was blinded on the Russian front, but neither he nor his wife, a devout Catholic, has ever mentioned anything about the depredations of the Nazis. In New York, Rosemarie became best friends with a girl in her office who was Jewish. One day they went to a beach, and while they sunbathed they looked at a magazine together. In it there was an article, with pictures, about the holocaust. Rosemarie stared at her friend and asked, 'Is this what you think of my people? How can you ever talk to me? I know that I could never have anything to do with someone who killed my parents.' Like Christina, she is in therapy, struggling with the problems of how to face her parents and her country when her job comes to an end.'

(4) "Dietrich S., thirty, a theology student from Hannover; he was in America for a year, taking special courses at a seminary.

"Dietrich has stated, 'Soon after arriving, I found myself in a room filled with some of the most distinguished names of Germany's former intellectual world. They were people who spoke the same language I did but claimed total dissociation from my country. It filled me with a sense of deep sorrow. I kept asking myself, How could any country afford the loss of those minds and talents? Several weeks later, I was invited to attend a panel discussion of the Warsaw ghetto uprising. It was

110

held to mark the thirtieth anniversary of that event. Films were shown that I had never seen before. I saw skeletons, thousands of them—human bodies that no longer had anything human about them—being scooped up by a bulldozer and thrown into a mass grave. I was the only German present. I was tempted to tell everyone in the audience that I came from Sweden or Denmark, but it would have been no use. The image of that bulldozer has yet to leave me. I am a German."

I did not acknowledge Mrs. Hershan's second communication in writing. I spoke with her directly. I asked her a single question: How had she ever gotten into her study? She attributed it to her husband's death, several years ago. At loose ends then, she had taken a job as manager of the German section of an international bookshop on Fifth Avenue. She had held the job three years, in which interval, she estimated, she had become acquainted with well over 1,000 Germans, most of them young and all intending to go home again. She recalled for me her meeting with one of the first of these book hunters. He had complimented her on her German, and, coldly, impersonally, she had let him know it was her native tongue.

"Why did you leave your country?" he asked.

"Hitler—you've heard of him, haven't you?"

"Yes, but not much—and that was so long ago, wasn't it?"

"When were you born?"

"Nineteen-fifty."

Interchanges like that, which occurred repeatedly, had

an effect on her, Mrs. Hershan told me. She began to have young Germans over to her apartment, alone or in groups, to talk about the Third Reich; occasionally, she had refugees like herself over, thus bringing together children of post-Hitler Germany and, in her words, "victims of their fathers." Her Teutonic guests reciprocated, introducing her to fellow nationals; frequently, on returning to Germany, they advised friends, about to leave for America, to look up Mrs. Hershan at the bookshop. Throughout, Mrs. Hershan said, she kept careful records of the shock of discovery that her young acquaintances were experiencing; but things weren't all one way, she remarked, for the more she saw of them, the more she found that she was capable of liking Germans, at least those away from Europe. That was something she hadn't anticipated. Since coming to America, she had avoided Germans; indeed, she and her late husband had abjured the use of the German language. It is a long time now since Mrs. Hershan resigned her post at the bookshop, but she remains in touch with Germans. She wants to keep alive the measure of mutual sentience—of connection—she has known with them; its spark, she thinks, may have something to do with keeping the future, theirs and hers, from being entirely dark.